A Time for Volunteers

From Papua New Guinea to the
Townsville Floods

James R. Byrne

Copyright © 2025 by James R. Byrne

All rights reserved.

No portion of this book may be reproduced in any form without written permission from the publisher or author.

Contents

Prologue	1
1. Today's Storm, Yesterday's Lessons	5
2. The Time That Was Before	22
3. Papua New Guinea Part I – Milne Bay and Oro Bay	37
4. Papua New Guinea Part II – The Village and the Port	75
5. The Distant Thunder of Paluma	94
6. The Surge in the Streets	104
7. By First Light	118
8. The Long Week of the Leviathan	135
9. The Rise of Team Townsville	144
10. When the Waters Withdrew	161
11. Volunteering Beyond	170
12. Farewell, Olden Ways	180
Acknowledgements	192
From the author	193

Prologue

Many stories start with "Once upon a time," laying out a familiar path with a clear beginning, a structured middle, and a defined end. These stories often unfold as if they exist in a vacuum, detached from the complex realities of life. The opening scene paints a picture of a world untouched by what's to come. A world that seems simple.

However, stories like those below, ones of reality, have a different path. They can hardly fit in the neat confines of a tidy narrative. These stories don't just unfold. They unravel, intertwined with the threads of history. In these tales, the beginning is more than just a starting point; it's a consequence of what has come before, a reflection of choices made, and paths not taken. The middle isn't just a series of events leading to a conclusion, instead it is a journey through the unknown. The end is never really the end, but rather a transition, a momentary pause before the next chapter begins.

When I walk alone by the shore, the last light of day long gone, I can still hear those stories of the past in my personal reflections. They had taken place under those stars, ebbing and flowing like the waves of the ocean. This is one of those stories, on my own voyage through the sea of time...

Stories about disasters, like the ones covered here, do not simply happen. They are triggered by a chain of events. To understand such a story, one must unravel the clues, fateful decisions, and factors that set them in motion...

In the last year of the 2010s, a major flood event struck the city of Townsville and the surrounding areas of North Queensland. Since its settlement in the 1860s, Townsville has endured around twenty major flooding events. Prime examples among them were from Cyclone Yasi in 2011, just eight years earlier, the 1998 Night of Noah, and Cyclone Althea in 1971. In spite of that, this event has become one of the worst natural disasters to ever impact the region and will surely remain so for a long time.

Or so I still hope.

As of this writing, four years have passed since the floods. It may very well be more as of your reading. The greater community has long since moved on as the wheels of time keep turning. To this day, for many, the wounds the floods left behind continue to run deep until they finally heal. Many people worked hard to recover their homes, while others lost theirs entirely. The floods are now a notorious chapter in Townsville's long history of battles against the extremes of heavy flooding and long droughts.

Some evidence of their endeavours still remains, but not much. It lingers, like the afterglow of a light after it's turned off.

As tragic as that may be, it is equalled by many stories of volunteers, people who were willing to answer the city calling for help and assist their fellow citizens in their time of need. Many of the locals volunteered to assist emergency services, evacuating trapped residents by boat from their flooded homes. The considerable number of volunteers, boats, and resulting queue of helpers earned their name in history as the Tinnie Army of Battlefield Queensland.

A TIME FOR VOLUNTEERS

As a witness of the flood event and a volunteer during its aftermath, I felt compelled to share my own story, knowing that countless others have also shared their experiences. By sharing my perspective, I hope to contribute to a more comprehensive and unclouded understanding of the event. It is my sincerest wish that through these accounts, the true impact and the indomitable spirit of the people affected by this disaster will be recognized and celebrated.

As one will later see, however, this was just another chapter in the long story of the local community spirit.

It would be fair to say I have witnessed some modern history in Townsville since being born and raised in this vibrant city in 1997. Growing up here has shaped me into the person I am today with a deep connection to the community. My educational journey started at Townsville Central State School where I joined the Class of 2009. Those early years of learning and exploration laid the foundation for my intellectual curiosity. I always felt a bit different, with a special mind that yearned for knowledge and a desire to break free from the constraints of ordinary life. This mindset carried on as I progressed to Townsville State High School, graduating with the Class of 2014. It was during my high school years that I fully embraced my individuality and my unique qualities.

A lot of places I have visited have long since moved on. There are few things more desolate, I feel, than places once familiar, now empty or abandoned. I would keep visiting Townsville Central State School well after my school years were concluded. The old YWAM building on Ingham Road that I would go to has long transformed into another business. Going back to these places, however, activates a nostalgic feeling. It can unlock memories long lost that you thought you left behind. It takes you back to times you perceived as simpler. Even so, the more you can look back and think how far away it was, the more you have progressed in life.

I saw chapters begin and end. I watched the visitors come and go, and I kept on my own path. So many young souls visited or stayed within this community on their own adventures around the city, the big country or the wider world. I have seen them around and would listen to their stories, hoping others would hear them too.

Chapter One

Today's Storm, Yesterday's Lessons

It was the first day of February 2025.

I had woken from one of the best sleeps I'd had in a while. Deep, uninterrupted, and peaceful. From my raising eyes, my view expanded to my dark room, illuminated by the faint glow of an overcast sky beyond the curtains. I had emerged from the kind of sleep that feels like it improved something mentally, which was the aim of the gap year I was currently in following a rough year of advanced study. The peace was made better by the rain on the roof. An old, familiar sound that wrapped the night and morning in calm.

My dream that night, made better by my peaceful state of mind, was vivid, imaginative, alive with colour. A world inside that I had observed and followed since my early childhood days. I had been exploring potential futures in my writing, walking with characters I hadn't fully created yet, weaving stories that blended science fiction with an olden twist. It had felt purposeful, inspired. One of those rare creative visions that left me eager to write, which I have followed for quite some time. Hopefully, I can share it with you, the reader, in time and in some form.

Then, I leant over and grabbed my charged phone. It was sitting as I had left it while serving its role of reading audiobooks last night. I checked it, and the screen bore a text message that, in a single moment, turned the mood of the day. The messages from the Townsville Local Disaster Management Group had shifted in tone. At 11:36AM, while I was unashamedly sleeping in, a text message came that told me everything had changed:

"Cluden, Hermit Park, Idalia, Oonoonba, Railway Estate and Rosslea. Dangerous flooding is expected in the next 24hrs. You must PREPARE TO LEAVE."

Oh, boy, I thought... *Here we go again...*

This was a clear departure from the cautious phrasing of before which read *"Prepare to leave if you are experiencing flooding and feel unsafe."* This was no longer a maybe. It was a must.

I had seen this before. We all had. When the rains first came, most of us wanted to believe it was just another wet season burst. A few days of inconvenience, and then "She'll be right, mate." In no time, we would be getting on with the day, to work, to rest. But now, as the alerts grew stronger and the warnings became sharper, it was apparent this wasn't passing. It was building, and it wasn't going to stop.

So, I did what I had done in the past, during other long days and nights. I broke out the log again, where I put down what I see, feel, hear. It was like a bunker journal, because that's what my home had become again. A shelter from the storm.

And so, away we went...

By three in the afternoon, it felt like things had indeed escalated. The trees outside were flowing and whooshing like stormy waves breaking on a beach, their limbs caught in the rhythm of something older and more powerful than wind. They swayed back and forth with slow, sweeping motions, like sea anemones underwater, bending with invisible currents that pulsed through the air.

The rain hadn't let up. If anything, it had found new power, sweeping across the sky in long grey streaks, hammering the rooftops and flattening the grass. Gusts of wind howled through the air with the voice of something wild and watchful. The pressure began to tighten. Not just the weather, but the knowledge. The steady tick of time, symbolised by the old clock in the living room, dragging us closer to something we couldn't fully see yet. My phone buzzed on the table. Another alert, another reminder.

There was a calm before the storm, yes. This wasn't it. This was the storm learning to breathe.

Fortunately, we'd learned some hard lessons from past extreme weather. 2019 wasn't so far behind us that the muscle memory had faded. I'd taken advantage of that knowledge in the moment, as I checked the emergency management dashboard, eyes scanning for updates. The Townsville Local Disaster Management Group had moved to "Stand Up," the highest state of local readiness before full-scale disaster response. That meant no one was treating this as just another heavy wet season anymore. Resources were mobilised; personnel activated. Everyone was on deck. The Local Disaster Co-ordination Centre had been stood up too. It was game on!

Community alerts reminded us to keep our radios on, to monitor the dashboard, to know our plans, to have our kits by the door. The latest bulletin from Townsville City Council confirmed it: Beaches and rivers closed, evacuation preparation notices in effect. Residents of Cluden, Hermit Park, Idalia, Oonoonba, Railway Estate, and Rosslea had to prepare to leave.

I opened the TLDMG map. A thick Pink Zone shaded much of the city's southern stretch – Dalrymple Road, parts of Thuringowa, Garbutt, West End, even the CBD. But it was the Black Zone cutting right along the Ross River and sweeping through the most vulnerable suburbs that sent the real alarm bells going. That was a lot of city at risk...

And yet, even in all that, I held on to the little things ahead. A notification told me that *Within Temptation* was coming to Brisbane when I'd already planned to see *Alestorm* that week. Hell of a pairing: symphonic metal and pirate shanties. Even if I had to get there by ark, I wasn't missing it. Because that's the thing about this city. About its people. Even with water rising and skies brooding, we still look for the light ahead, whatever shape it takes. The deep dive in discographies was the music getting me through the dark rainy night.

That night, after wrestling with a full-blown ant invasion, because apparently nature wasn't finished with me yet, I slumped back onto the couch, tired but wired. The rain had become a constant presence, its rhythm on the roof both soothing and ominous. I glanced at my phone again out of habit, not expecting much. And there it was.

"Emergency Warning – Cluden, Hermit Park, Idalia, Oonoonba, Railway Estate & Rosslea. Dangerous flooding will occur. LEAVE BY MIDDAY SUN 2 FEB to evacuate safely."

Now that was quite the escalation.

No more hedging or maybes. No more *"prepare to leave if you feel unsafe."* This was direct and blunt. Just like that, it felt like 2019 again. Déjà vu with a side of unease. That year carved itself into our collective memory, from the monsoonal siege to the flooding and the weeks of recovery. And now, this was shaping up to be its sequel. Same suburbs, rising tension, and the river swelling past its seams.

I sat in silence for a moment. That was a lot of ground to clear. A lot of people. A lot of unknowns. At times, I wonder if the concern I have in moments like these is legitimate or just part of my own anxiety.

Outside, the rain kept falling. Unrelenting, steady, like waves in the sky rolling across an invisible ocean. The streets, the gutters and the roofs were all part of the same vast current now.

Tomorrow, it seemed, would be a day of decisions. And for now, all I could do was get some rest, if I could. Because even storms give way to dawn... eventually.

The following morning, North Ward was covered in an almost ethereal grey overcast. The rain seemed to be lighter than it was last night, but the wind continued its series of squalls.

I had to hear what local radio was saying, so I tuned in to ABC Radio Queensland...

A severe weather warning remained in effect for heavy, locally intense rainfall and damaging winds over Northeast Queensland. Heavy rainfall, which would lead to flash flooding, was forecast between Tully and Ayr, extending inland to the far eastern Northern Goldfields and Upper Flinders. Additionally, locally intense rainfall, capable of causing dangerous, life-threatening flash flooding, was possible between Cairns and Townsville. Isolated to scattered showers and thunderstorms were expected across most of the state tomorrow.

With the devastating 2019 Townsville flood still fresh in memory, it was hard to believe we were back here so soon. Statistically, the 2019 event was considered rare, yet we were to face another flood of similar magnitude. At this stage, it was difficult to predict the full extent of the situation.

The Herbert River remained in an especially dire situation. For the Haughton River, authorities predicted that flood levels would approach those recorded in March 2018, with major flooding already occurring along the river. Hourly updates continued throughout the afternoon as part of ongoing emergency coverage. In situations like cyclones or major floods, real-time monitoring is essential. The radio would be tracking the rising river levels and the movement of the tropical low off the coast hour by hour.

All schools in Townsville and the Hinchinbrook local government areas would be closed the following day due to localised flooding. Residents in flood-affected areas were urged to prioritise their safety. The most severe flooding had affected communities around Townsville, Innisfail, Ingham, Gordonvale, and Cardwell, as well as all flood-impacted regions in North and Far North Queensland since 29 January.

The rainfall across Northeast Queensland had been truly incredible, with some areas exceeding 1,000 millimetres of rain. Given these extreme totals, it was no surprise that dangerous and major flooding was impacting many communities, including Townsville and Ingham. The severe weather warning remained in effect, and heavy rainfall was expected to continue for at least the next 18 to 24 hours.

A severe thunderstorm warning was issued, particularly affecting Paluma, where rainfall intensity had been extreme. Heavy rainfall was concentrated north of Bluewater, stretching up toward Rollingstone and the Bruce Highway. Strong winds were converging along this portion of the coastline, creating extremely dangerous and life-threatening flash flooding risks, especially in Paluma and Rollingstone.

The most immediate concern was the ongoing heavy rainfall pushing down toward Magnetic Island and Townsville that afternoon. Converging storm bands from the Coral Sea were forming intense rain trains, stretching from Dunk Island to Charters Towers.

Then, Bluewater Creek hit major flood levels. This was new information added to the severe thunderstorm warning, emphasising the risk of catastrophic flash flooding due to a particularly severe thunderstorm cell over Paluma, with 173 millimetres falling in just three hours before 2:00PM that day. A severe weather warning remained in effect for heavy, locally intense rainfall and damaging winds from Tully to Ayr, potentially continuing into early next week and inland to the Northern Goldfields and Upper Flinders, including Charters Towers. Mount Garnet residents had reported ominous black storm clouds rolling in. Rainfall in the Ravenshoe and Mount Garnet area was a serious concern as this region formed the upper catchment of the Herbert River, meaning all additional rainfall would flow downstream, compounding the already critical flood situation.

Around three in the afternoon, I decided to step out for a walk, grabbing my binoculars and my Achievement Hunter umbrella. The view at the far end of Stanton Terrace was what I sought as that could give me a better view of the rest of the city.

It was a route long familiar to me; one I used to walk well before I had a car. Down it I'd go for events at the YWAM campus, to the gym, delivering pamphlets door-to-door, or simply to move, to breathe. Each step on that pavement carried echoes of different seasons in my life. I'd listened to audiobooks from Ernest Hemingway to the *Tomorrow* series, then Tom Clancy and Matthew Reilly. Music too, from epic instrumentals to symphonic metal, all swirling in my ears as I walked. Not the sort of soundtrack you'd typically find in someone's daily commute, but then again, I've never been what you'd call typical.

Today added a new chapter to that.

The drainage channels were alive with water, rushing and frothing as they always do in storms. Tree branches drooped low under the weight of the rain, casting long shadows. As I climbed the hill, a hush fell over the world. No cars. No other people. Just me, the steady patter of rain, and the stillness save for my footsteps. It felt like being dropped into the world of a video game, something like *Halo* or *Skyrim*, those quiet moments between locations of action. Visually, it resembled the remaster of a survival game, the textures richer, the lighting more cinematic, as if reality itself had been subtly re-rendered. Come to think of it, life is basically a large open-world game anyhow...

Eventually, I veered off toward the service road leading to the old water tanks by the Maidenhair Track. An alternate viewpoint. As the road turned to dirt and the smell that of grass, I could just make out the floodplain, patched in shades of grey, green, and murky brown. Beyond the Ross River, the wetlands shimmered under the veil of rain. Some bodies of water belonged there. Others didn't. The roads below were sparse, empty save for a few collected vans and vehicles gathered near Reid Park.

Then the rain picked up again, gentle but steady. A cue, perhaps. I turned back the way I came, letting the sensation of it wash over me. In the stillness and silence, I felt it all again: the weight of memory, the quiet defiance of nature, the ever-persistent rhythm of a place I knew, and the strange comfort of being a witness to it all. Dervla McTiernan's *The Rúin* was sitting in the wooden box that was the local street library, which served as my read through it.

I made it back home just in time for more news on ABC Radio Queensland. The news continued... From the Burdekin to the Ross and Haughton, all the way down to the Pioneer River, a generalised flood watch extended to places like Charters Towers. Flooding was also seen for the South Johnston and the Mulgrave Rivers up towards Gordonvale. The Herbert River flooding approached 1967 levels, as well as March 2018 levels at Glen Eagle.

Levels comparable to 2009 were being reached at the Halifax and Burdekin Rivers, with flooding occurring at Sellheim that afternoon. Flooding was expected or already happening at Giru where a resident reported conditions just outside the town, noting significant inland ocean-like flooding.

The Ross and Bohle Rivers were in major flood. The Ross River was likely to hit the major flood level of 1.8 metres at Aplins Weir that afternoon with the potential to rise as high as 2 metres, depending on how much rain fell in the catchment. Flooding was occurring at Euramo, and likely at Murray Flats that afternoon.

Amidst all of this, while I was at home reading my new book, a new story was emerging elsewhere. Another one of a community coming together... Let me tell you about Euramo, a small rural locality nestled within the heart of the Cassowary Coast, a region known for its stunning natural beauty and rich agricultural land. With a modest population of just 114 residents, Euramo offers a sense of community and tranquillity that larger towns often lack.

Bounded to the north by the flowing Tully River and to the south by the tranquil Murray River, the locality benefits from its proximity to these vital water sources. The rivers not only provide scenic beauty but also support the local ecosystem, contributing to the area's agricultural activities and overall landscape.

The Bruce Highway cuts through the eastern part of Euramo from the direction of Murrigal and continues its journey north-east to Silky Oak. In addition to the highway, the North Coast railway line runs just to the west of the Bruce Highway, adding to Euramo's strategic location.

During this historic flooding event, a story from Euramo would spread far and wide across North Queensland. A tale of resilience, mateship, and a community refusing to be beaten by the rising waters.

Once again, the pop-up 'yacht club' emerged as a beacon of defiance, rallying the locals together in the face of adversity.

For the second time in just over a year, Hotel Euramo stood its ground against the encroaching floodwaters, refusing to close its doors when the community needed it most. As the Cassowary Coast battled yet another bout of wild weather, the iconic pub became more than just a watering hole. It became a refuge, a meeting place, and a symbol of the unwavering North Queensland spirit.

Despite the floodwaters swirling around them, the pub remained open throughout the weekend, with locals finding a way to arrive by boat, docking their vessels right at the front door. It was an extraordinary sight, apparently. Boats tied up where cars would normally park, their owners wading through the water just for the comfort of a cold pint and a chat with friends.

The Euramo Yacht Club, as it had affectionally been dubbed after previous floods, had once again taken shape, not in defiance of the crisis, but as a celebration of the unbreakable community spirit that defines life in the tropics. Through the chaos, laughter echoed across the water, glasses clinked in solidarity, and the bonds of mateship only grew stronger.

In tough times, communities either pull apart or pull together. Euramo's residents had chosen the latter, not by running from the floodwaters, but by rowing straight into them, with a beer in hand and a smile on their faces.

Such was the previous edition of the Euramo Yacht Club in December of 2023, just after Tropical Cyclone Jasper, when they had flooding that made headlines. Today though, they had a few little showers, nothing heavy, and a little bit of wind, but for the most part, the day had been relatively calm. That was encouraging news.

It seemed that the Euramo Hotel was doing well, and it was clear that the local residents were making the most of their afternoon, gathering together with a strong sense of community. Their properties hadn't had a lot of water, so they enjoyed the moment, sharing drinks and enjoying the close-knit spirit.

As the day progressed, more reports came in. The Burdekin Bridge was now closed, cutting Townsville off. Giru remained in immediate danger. Authorities were urging residents to follow their evacuation plans and seek shelter with family or friends in designated safe zones. An emergency warning remained in place for six Townsville suburbs under evacuation orders. The Queensland Police Service and the Australian Defence Force were continuing to evacuate homes in the so-called Black Zone, where authorities warned flooding was inevitable. Evacuees had little time to prepare, grabbing only small bags of clothes and irreplaceable treasures like family photos. However, many remained hopeful, saying, "You can always start again."

As darkness fell, I decided to take a break from listening to the radio, having heard enough important and useful information for now. The breaks in the rain were gone now, and it fell once more. Grey clouds swirled in the heavens. A heavy sense of loneliness came over me.

My home city was under threat, and there was not much I could do to prevent it. I did not like being unable to do anything or help anyone. I hoped I could share this story, or any story, with the wider community. I still hadn't published my book of the previous major floods like I hoped I would last year. Would many people read it anyway? Will my vision really be shared? Questions like these kept tugging at my mind even during something like this. I always tended to be restless anyhow...

On the third day, the floods continued to rise across parts of North Queensland. There were eleven rescues overnight with the SES having fielded almost five hundred calls for assistance in the past 24 hours. Severe weather warnings remained current for parts of the North Tropical Coast, the Tablelands and the Herbert and Lower Burdekin. Townsville residents were being warned that floodwaters were expected to peak in the city the following morning, with 1700 homes in the so-called Black Zone at risk. The Queensland Premier said the ADF had been approached for aerial support. The Defence Forces were on standby and had agreed overnight to the use of some of their assets if required. Emergency alerts were also current for two regions on the Cassowary Coast.

The Weather Bureau said there was likely to be a gradual weakening of the low-pressure system at the centre of the flooding disaster. That rainfall was expected to ease over, but there was a lot of water in those catchments and already an incredible mass of water on the ground. There was more significant rain to come, so it would take days for that water to come out of those systems.

In the days ahead, while I carried on with the rhythm of a city still drenched and dazed, the headlines began to piece together a wider picture, threads of a tapestry woven from hardship and resilience.

On the 7th of March, I read in the paper that food and water were being flown into Ingham, a town slowly beginning to pick up the pieces. The Premier pledged to fix what was broken in North Queensland. A promise made in the mud and ruin. Meanwhile, more grocery convoys rolled in as the Australian Defence Force began the delicate process of restoring the damaged Bruce Highway.

The Bruce Highway? Under work? At least there was still some normalcy there.

By the 10th, stories from the flood's ground zero painted a portrait of spirit and absurdity coexisting. A front-page image showed two blokes, waist-deep in floodwater, playing a game of pool on a floating table outside a pub in Ingham; A strange and endearing sight of grim waters made light with laughter and stubbornness. The kind only North Queenslanders could pull off.

But beyond the levity, the damage was stark. Roads were gone, cut away by rising rivers. Paluma, usually an emerald tropical retreat in the hills, had become an isolated pocket of crisis. Businesses cried out for help after floods wiped out access, drowned vital equipment, and left them severed from both supplies and communication. Hidden Valley Cabins, a beloved spot tucked in the rainforest, had been forced to cancel every booking. Tens of thousands in losses. They weren't alone.

Relief came in the most cinematic way imaginable: A Republic of Singapore Air Force CH-47F Chinook touched down outside Ingham State High School, offloading pallets of supplies. That image in the paper was a snapshot from a region fighting to breathe again. Chinooks from Singapore aren't unusual here, for they train with the ADF in the tropics. But this was not a drill.

The wet season of 2025 was long and restless, unfolding in waves and tempests, like waking from one dream into another during a long night, each more vivid and unpredictable than the last.

Northeastern Queensland experienced major flooding across three key periods: late January, early February, and mid-March. The disaster claimed at least two confirmed lives due to floodwaters, and an additional sixteen deaths were linked to a disease outbreak that followed. Mass evacuations were ordered across coastal communities, and the floods were estimated to have caused $1.2 billion in economic damage across Queensland.

The Shire of Hinchinbrook, home to around 11,000 residents, was among the hardest-hit regions. Severe flooding also impacted suburbs of nearby Townsville, with Giru suffering significantly.

The Ross River Dam had reached 163.8% of its capacity. Authorities promptly closed the area to the public and restricted access. Further north, floodwaters caused the collapse of the Ollera Creek Bridge along the Bruce Highway, cutting off a vital artery for supplies and isolating several communities.

Ollera Creek, once just another crossing along the highway, was now a known name. Plans for a temporary bridge were underway, the kind of makeshift lifeline that says, "We'll get there, eventually." In response, the federal government deployed the Australian Defence Force to work alongside Queensland's Department of Transport and Main Roads on a temporary fix. Both the Prime Minister and the Queensland Premier publicly committed to rebuilding the bridge to higher standards for future resilience.

In Cardwell, floods submerged residential zones, prompting the Cassowary Coast Regional Council to issue emergency warnings for low-lying areas. In Ingham, widespread flooding forced businesses to close and roads to be blocked off. One man was rescued by locals from a submerged vehicle. Approximately 6,700 properties lost electricity after the Ingham Substation was shut down for safety.

The Herbert River surged to around fifteen metres which was a level not recorded since Cyclone Dinah in March 1967. Palm Island suffered a complete blackout after a landslide damaged its electrical infrastructure.

Then, on 19 March, a new surge of flooding struck again. Townsville and its surrounding communities faced renewed rainfall, with Toolakea recording the highest total of 293mm in a short period. Essential services across North Queensland were again disrupted. Over 8,000 homes lost power: approximately 6,000 in Hinchinbrook, 2,000 in Townsville, and 600 in Mackay.

Following that, Severe Tropical Cyclone Alfred, a powerful, long-lived, and erratic system, brought widespread impacts to Southeast Queensland and the New South Wales north coast. As the seventh named storm and sixth severe tropical cyclone of the 2024–25 Australian region cyclone season, Alfred originated from a tropical low in the Coral Sea on 20 February.

Widely anticipated as one of the most significant weather events in recent Australian history, Alfred prompted cyclone watches, warnings, and evacuation orders across Southeast Queensland and Northern New South Wales. Those regions rarely experience direct tropical cyclone impacts. Though Alfred weakened into a tropical low before making landfall on 8 March, it still delivered intense rainfall that triggered severe flooding across the affected regions.

On that day, as Cyclone Alfred began to weaken over cooler waters, the news highlighted how local heroes were already stepping up as the storm unleashed its fury across Southeast Queensland. Lifeguards, doctors, and SES personnel standing together. These are the everyday heroes who reflect the quintessential Queensland spirit. You'll find them in our suburbs, patrolling our beaches, and navigating floodwaters in boats. Some wear uniforms, others simply lend a hand however they can, often risking their own safety to protect others.

But the danger wasn't over yet. The following day, news warned of a life-threatening 48-hour deluge ahead. Adding to the gravity, several soldiers en route to assist with disaster response were injured in a crash. Cyclone Alfred returned for a punishing second round late Saturday night, battering Brisbane's northside and Redcliffe with Category 1 winds reaching 100 kilometres per hour. Thousands of homes were plunged into darkness as power lines fell. In Alfred's wake, a massive 400-kilometre-wide storm system was forecast to unload up to 700 millimetres of rain in just two days, setting the stage for dangerous, life-threatening flash floods across the region.

At least one fatality had been confirmed as a result of the cyclone, with four individuals reported missing. Several others sustained injuries, most notably in a road collision involving Australian Defence Force personnel at the height of the storm. The cyclone caused another estimated $1.2 billion in economic losses, adding further strain to communities already grappling with prior flooding events earlier in the year.

Furthermore, this wet season was gruelling for me mentally. In between the flood season and Cyclone Alfred, I would indeed have a great time at those concerts, feeling positivity and inspiration with *Within Temptation* at the Princess Theatre and having fun with *Alestorm* at the Tivoli. Alfred just in time, I'd come home to find my Uncle Peter, a musically talented, whimsical fellow, had surrendered to his poor health and passed on. Watching my city and state endure such relentless disasters, while also facing personal loss in other parts of my life, turned it into a true test of endurance. Even now, I still feel drained by it at times.

And yet, amid all the chaos and heartbreak, there was light. I saw neighbours helping neighbours, strangers reaching out across floodwaters, and entire communities rallying together with a quiet kind of heroism. In the face of power outages, damaged homes, and shattered routines, people showed up, not just out of duty, but out of deep care for one another. Volunteers worked through heat and rain, often with nothing more than a shovel, a wheelbarrow, and a desire to help. SES crews and firefighters went out day after day, while others cooked meals, lent out tools, or simply offered a warm smile and a listening ear.

It reminded me that while the elements can bring us to our knees, they can also reveal our greatest strengths. The resilience of Queenslanders is no small thing; It's lived out in the muddy boots, the tired hands, the flood maps shared online, and the quiet acts of generosity that occasionally make news. Even now, as I continue to recover, mentally, emotionally, and spiritually, I hold onto these glimpses of unity and courage. They are proof that even in the darkest wet season, even when the rain doesn't seem to stop, there are still people who will step forward and carry the weight together. And that gives me hope. It always will.

Sometimes I wonder if others feel it too, this strange mixture of sorrow and resilience, of being shaken but not alone. I think they do. Maybe they just don't have the words yet. Maybe that's what I'm here for, to put to paper the things we all carry in silence.

If that's true, then maybe there's a kind of purpose in all of this after all...

Yet, this whole story was not without precedent. The lessons of this wet season were not learned in isolation, nor were the responses forged entirely in the present.

In many ways, this was the sequel to another storm, the great deluge of 2019. The scars of that flood had not fully faded; they were etched into infrastructure, policy, and memory. But they also laid the groundwork for what followed. Emergency protocols were refined, response times improved, and local knowledge, hard-won and deeply felt, guided the decisions of today.

As the rainclouds began to drift and the sun cut once more through the grey, I found myself remembering where it all began. Before the Bruce Highway broke, before the helicopters came, before the water swallowed the paddocks and the roads turned to rivers, there was 2019.

Let me take you back...

Chapter Two

The Time That Was Before

The 2019 floods came at an interesting time for me. At the turn of the year, I was struggling for work. My Diploma of Aviation, which I had chosen in my final year of high school back in 2014, was impressive on paper, but practically invisible in the local job market by the time I graduated in 2018. It was a tough era, marked by a surge in youth unemployment. Like many others, I found myself in limbo, a qualified graduate in a region where opportunities seemed to vanish just as you reached out for them.

I went through the businesses of the airport, among other places, résumé in hand. But time and again, I was met by closed doors and polite rejections. I even remember approaching one business right as they were preparing to lay people off. It was that kind of luck. In the end, it wasn't a lack of drive, but a lack of experience. That elusive edge.

Still, I wasn't ready to sit idle. With the help of an employment agent, I signed up to volunteer at the Community Information Centre. I needed something that could offer a foothold, a place to start building from.

Nowadays, the CIC takes up a prominent space in Flinders Street, but when I started, it was in an office in a corner of the second floor, opposite to the Townsville City Library.

I have many memories of that floor. As a child, my father and grandmother would often take me to the library, and we would borrow anything from books to VHS tapes and cassettes. The VHS tapes were a range of content, from documentaries about steam trains and ships, to animated adaptations of classic children's books. Among them were *The Rainbow Serpent* by Dick Roughsey, *The Beast of Monsieur Racine* by Tomi Ungerer, and one of the biblical stories, *Jonah and the Great Fish*. Some I have since found resurfaced on YouTube archive channels.

One cassette tape series that truly sparked something in me were the stories by Kym Lardner. These were fictional, comedic tales drawn from his childhood, often beginning with "When I was only three..." delivered with his remarkable vocal flair and storytelling charm. One day, he toured Townsville, my primary school among them, and talking with him was what truly started my storytelling passion.

These tapes and stories, along with other media I explored at home and in the library, shaped a childhood that was already quite neurodivergent into something even more unique. I wasn't just absorbing stories; I was living in them. From the whimsical chaos of *Looney Tunes*, to the quiet wonder of a *Tales of Magic* anime series, I saw and took in narrative in all its forms.

Looking back, I realise these early encounters with storytelling weren't just entertainment. They were foundational. They helped me see the world differently, taught me rhythm and character, and stirred the early embers of my desire to create stories of my own.

Now here I was, adding to those memories in that building. It was quiet for the most part, and my duties were usually going on the shopping and mail run, preparing the various refreshments for the meetings I never saw, and general computer work. I still feel nostalgia for the creaking of the locker, the faint smell of dust and coffee, and finding a whole heap of floppy disks left from times before. Later on, that would give way to the smell of cooking Japanese food in the lobby and the hustle of the various surrounding offices.

For two years, I enjoyed it very much. It was there that I could continue being a volunteer for my city, while improving my experience in office work. There, people continue to help and support others who have been affected by natural disasters. As an example, I was there when the Emergency Management and Disaster Dashboard was revealed, and which I would use during Cyclone Kirrily's day. Stories, experiences, and other things to share have appeared over the course of time. Some were small, and some were long. Some were of personal lives, and others were of businesses coping with the sudden change of events.

Over time, the picture of the City of Townsville, being one proud of its abilities to handle extremes, became quite clear. Sure, many outside it knew that the city faced a few challenges other than simply the weather, but it is still my home, and I'll take it any day. Located in the dry tropics of this massive Australian continent, Townsville depends on seasonal monsoons to maintain its water supply. These monsoons are vital to our way of life, but they sometimes come with a price.

The way Townsville responds to major weather events has become part of its collective character. I have heard some people say that community acceptance of recurrent, but unpredictable major weather events has not led to the development of a sustainable flood memory;

that these floods demonstrate that although Townsville often experiences heavy rains, it has failed to foster a communal memory and understanding of how to live with flooding.

To those people, I must ask... Are you certain of that? I feel compelled to challenge that assertion indeed. The people who have experienced the floods of 2019, 2011, 1998, and even cyclones like Althea, Yasi, Debbie, and Jasper are not likely to forget the impact and devastation caused by these events. Even Kirrily served as a fresh reminder of that. The memory of these disasters remains deeply ingrained in the collective consciousness of the community.

In fact, the resilience of the Townsville community in the face of natural adversity demonstrates the strength of our communal memory. People have come together time and again to support and rebuild, forming bonds and strategies to better prepare for future challenges. The lessons learned from each event contribute to a growing understanding of how to live with and respond to flooding.

That, I believe, is my unique perspective. While it is true that no city is immune to the challenges of extreme weather, Townsville has developed mechanisms and systems to mitigate the impact and build resilience. The community has shown a remarkable ability to adapt, evolve, and learn from past experiences. The commitment to sustainable flood management practices, the implementation of flood warning systems, and the ongoing efforts to improve infrastructure are all evidence of Townsville's dedication to addressing the challenges posed by major weather events.

So, to those who doubt the sustainability of Townsville's flood memory, I invite them to speak with the residents who have lived through these events. The memories are vivid, and the commitment to preparedness and resilience is strong. Townsville continues to evolve and improve, drawing upon its collective experience to better navigate the challenges posed by nature. It is a city that is proud of its ability to handle extremes and remains determined to create a safer and more resilient future for its residents.

Or even better, maybe not so much speak to them as listen to what they have to say.

In 2024, as I was writing this very piece, I woke up to series of grey clouds building on the horizon over Magnetic Island. I remember the feeling from Cyclone Yasi, the calm before the coming storm. The wind did not feel like the gentle breeze, but an eerie quality. A true calm before the rising storm. We were just waiting for the clouds to fall. It was quiet all around.

Magnetic Island then disappeared behind a grey wall of water. The show had begun. I swiftly open Microsoft Word on my laptop and take position on the keyboard. The floods have taught me to archive my thoughts during events like these. They may come in handy later, for either telling a personal story or contributing to knowledge of the wider event...

It was the 25th of February again, around five years to the days of Paluma and the floods. Cyclone Kirrily was here. The Bureau of Meteorology warned the cyclone would bring more dangerous weather in coming hours with winds of up to 140 kilometres per hour. Locals had boarded up businesses and battened down the hatches in preparation for the Category 2 system, which was expected to intensify throughout the day before making landfall in Townsville.

Residents from Ingham to Hinchinbrook were being told to take shelter now, as destructive winds from Tropical Cyclone Kirrily lashed the region. Magnetic Island, Townsville and Palm Island residents were also told to stay inside. Queensland Premier Stephen Miles said a state of disaster had pre-emptively been declared. We were prepared and ready for the worst, now we waited and hoped for the best. The message to Queenslanders was that now is the time to make sure that you are ready, and make sure your emergency kit is topped up. The Mackay mayor was warning residents not to be complacent. Remember, these things could change. By this point, it was about 420 kilometres from Townsville, but changes could be caused by any movement a couple of degrees north or south, and then the whole scenario would change again. Cases of the potentially deadly disease melioidosis were also on the rise in the Cairns region after heavy rain and flooding.

I had sent a text to ABC Radio's text line. They responded shortly after, much to my excitement. At quarter to three, I had a conversation with the DJ. The enthusiastic producer put me through after hearing I was in the middle of writing a book about the 2019 Townsville floods. After finishing his conversation with the other person, I was put through. I told him about my view on my veranda, how there was indeed violent rain and wind, followed by a few deceptive patches of sunlight. He showed particular interest in my book, and I pointed out that the community spirit that I had seen in the 2019 Townsville floods was also present here for all to see. I said perhaps we will see the Tinnie Army make a comeback, which, as he correctly pointed out, "was a right cracker!" Perhaps it didn't come this time, but the new Chainsaw Army definitely made up for it. He wished me and the others well, and we concluded the chat. It was a shame that I had no recording equipment on me at the time. That was quite a proud moment. So, if you were listening to ABC radio around quarter to three on the day of the cyclone... Yes, that was me. Then, I felt like I had to finish the book...

And so, I did.

Prior to that, they were talking to people in the regions affected by Cyclone Debbie. There was still a bit of a hangover in that region. People remembered the community spirit. There was talk of something called the Chainsaw Army, which now that I think of it, sounded like something out a zombie apocalypse movie. Instead, it was a term for members of the local community who brought their chainsaws to prune fallen branches. "These names are just bizarre, aren't they?" was said over the radio, followed by "That's the big secret to the whole thing." They also spoke to someone working in their vehicle along the Woodstock-Giru Road. As I would see during a drive down there with my mate, David, that quiet corner of land called Majors Creek can be quite unstable, even during a normal monsoon.

The radio would continue on. Occasionally, they played something with some spirit. The DJ loved it. I share his feeling of being very proud to live in an area the songs from local artists come from. The community working together to get it all cleaned up. By the end of the day the streets were all cleaned and look like a million bucks.

As the day turned to dusk, the wind began to pick up. It was soon becoming a fury. The trees swayed back and forth with increasing violence. The hill was coming alive. When it didn't smell of moisture, the air was instead smelling of plants. A text I sent to ABC Radio that they read aloud warned of squall patterns. I said that it wasn't Yasi levels of bad – although it would be pretty close in my suburb. The eye was coming.

The new radio DJ described the storm. *"There's no other way to describe it and nothing I can say is going to take that away. But just know that everyone else that's listening to this right now is wishing you well whether you know it or not. The fact that people are tuning in from around Australia and I'm seeing texts piling up here from people tuning in in Victoria, South Australia, England. So just try to hold onto that. You'll get through this and then we'll start to clean up tomorrow."*

It's funny how everything old can become new again. For many of us, actually. We might have forgotten that this was how we used to ride out cyclones without all the modern technology, individually sitting around the radio, maybe playing some board games under candlelight. That was the way that we would have thought about preparing for a cyclone not that long ago. But now with all the modern technology, the battery chargers, the power banks and the like, you know, you could have downloaded probably four days' worth of shows if you had enough memory and not necessarily engage with the rest of your community via the radio, but why do that when they can be here with us?

As night fell, it was really starting to escalate. The wind was roaring. The trees were shaking and groaning louder than ever. There would usually be a few moments when it was gradually rough, followed by an even more powerful squall.

Suddenly, a green flash silently cracked through the suburb, and the houses, ours included, were plunged into darkness. We were all in the dark then. The only sources of light were some far away streetlights and traffic lights, but even those cut out at least twice, gradually returning shortly after.

Today's volunteering work was getting a broom and sweeping vegetation off verandas and paths. More close-to-home work than the floods, but I did what I could. Despite the heat, it was still a lovely, sunny day out. Around us was the stillness of midday accompanied by the occasional birdsong.

As I wrote in my blog back then, when a challenge does rise, there will always be a group of volunteers who stand to meet it. By helping communities in time of need, they also light the darkness. They will make the night less empty.

The cycle is as natural as the pattern made by the dust on a butterfly's wings. At times, we understand it no more than the butterfly does, and we do not know when our wings are brushed or marred. Later, some become conscious of their damaged wings and of their construction. That said, however, some become aware before they cannot fly anymore, but the love of flight remains in corners of the heart. Some, meanwhile, can only remember when it had been effortless....

Going back to 2019, the Townsville City Library presented a remarkable opportunity for individuals to share their stories and experiences, a commendable initiative that promised to elicit a multitude of inspiring and diverse responses to the question, "What did you do during the floods?" An amazing idea, for that question is guaranteed to inspire and generate many great answers.

If you feel like you don't have what it takes to share, you won't know until you try. Even if one story is all you have, the difference between one and zero is as great as one and infinity. No answer is too great or too small.

I've learned from listening to Irish folk music, and from the music choices of my late Uncle Peter, that there is more than one way to sing a tune. A tune can carry several versions, each one shaped by the singer's voice, the mood of the day, or the memory it carries. Storytelling is much the same. There isn't only one "correct" version of a story—there are as many as there are tellers. Each person brings a different cadence, a different emphasis, and a different life behind their words. That doesn't diminish the story; it enriches it.

That is the gentle wisdom in Irish folk music, a tradition that ripples through fields and hearths, past and present, reminding us: there is never just one way to sing a tune or tell a story. A melody, once born, weaves its path from heart to heart, gathering new flourishes with every voice that carries it. Sometimes, a song sounds mournful and slow; elsewhere, it is lilting and bright. No two renditions are ever exactly alike. This, I believe, is not only the beauty of folk music, but the essence of storytelling itself.

So, I want to encourage you: share your story in your own way. No two voices are the same, and that is exactly what makes the chorus so powerful.

Should you have a story or experience linked to this moment in local history, I wholeheartedly encourage you to share it in any form that feels right for you—be it through writing, speaking, or art. You can do it. It's absolutely possible to create something meaningful.

Just remember, there's no shortage of examples to draw inspiration from, myself included. Don't hesitate to make beginner mistakes; they're a natural part of the journey. We all start rough around the edges, especially if we're unfamiliar with tools, platforms, or even the basics of the craft, as I once was. The key is to have fun. In challenging times like these, every little bit of joy matters.

Should you aim high, just know that it takes patience, effort, trial and error, and occasional setbacks to find your rhythm. I can recall my early days making YouTube short films, pouring my heart into projects while juggling university and part-time work. Despite the hours I invested, my work often went unnoticed, a tough reality for a young creator.

Even bestselling authors I've listened, and sometimes spoken to, will affirm that the hours you dedicate won't always mirror your achievements. At first, your work might not receive much attention simply because it may not yet stand out. Rookie mistakes are inevitable, but they're also invaluable. They're stepping stones to finding your unique voice and perspective.

The more you can look back on earlier work and think, "Did I really create that?" the more it reflects your growth and progress. Feeling that your past efforts were less polished can be a sign of how far you've come.

If your work pays off, fantastic! Keep pushing forward, improving, and see where it goes. But if they don't, carry no regrets. Appreciate the experience and the journey itself, knowing that every attempt adds to something greater.

Because one thing that saddens me, more deeply than even I often acknowledge, is the idea of a forgotten story—a tale once carried with passion, purpose, or pain, now left untold. A lost piece of art that no one pauses to notice, no longer evoking gasps or wonder. A book gathering dust on a forgotten shelf, its words once so carefully chosen, now unread. A song once sung from the heart, now silent.

There's something quietly tragic about a story that no one hears. Stories are how we pass on who we are. They are the invisible threads that bind us across generations. And when they vanish, when no voice remains to carry them forward, something irreplaceable goes with them. A perspective is lost. A spark goes dim. A bridge to understanding collapses.

It reminds me why I write. Why I tell stories. Why I collect memories, record moments, and give voice to things that otherwise might fade. Because every story deserves a chance to live—even if only in a single reader's mind. And maybe, just maybe, by telling our stories, we make space for others to tell theirs too.

Because of this, the notion the library implied, that everyone has a unique narrative to contribute, is both empowering and resonant. It encourages individuals to step forward and share their perspectives, as the potential for greatness lies within every response, regardless of its perceived magnitude.

The library's invitation lingered in the air, and though I had initially heard whispers of it within the Community Information Centre, life's whirlwind momentarily caused me to forget. In the subsequent year of 2020, I recollected and seized the opportunity, penning a detailed account of my experiences during the infamous flood. Despite encountering delays in the platform's launch, a shared struggle in the face of contemporary challenges, I applaud the collective efforts that ultimately prevailed. To those who navigated the obstacles, my heartfelt congratulations.

Having said that, time had passed. It was no longer simply an end, but also a beginning. I felt it necessary to include more of my volunteering memories, such as Papua New Guinea and the CIC. Soon, the floods became just another chapter.

I've written this book during many a quiet moment. Often, it would be on a lonely couch at midnight, during another rainy day, or a peaceful afternoon. For the most part, the world around me was still and quiet. The only noises being a patter of rain on the roof, the gentle swaying of breezes in the greenery outside, or the classical instruments playing fantasy-themed tunes that served as my thinking music. The mood can feel heavy, almost sombre, especially when writing about events in a past that drifts further and further away in time. Sometimes it would become emotional later on. Every fond memory becomes more nostalgic. Every lesson learned becoming more valuable. Every picture of the event more of a window back to moments you felt in the foreground and the wider world in the background.

If you are seeking the perspective of an average citizen in the account that follows, I must offer a gentle disclaimer – you may not find it here. My journey through the Townsville floods was anything but ordinary, and my method of archiving and recounting these experiences is equally distinct. Average may be the norm, but normal is no fun anyways! What unfolds here is not merely my story; it is a unique thread woven into our collective narrative of the Townsville Floods. As I embark on sharing these unconventional experiences, I invite you to join me in exploring the extraordinary, for in the realm of the extraordinary lies the true essence of our shared story.

In crafting this story, I hope to shed light on the profound impact of volunteerism, transcending the boundaries of individual incidents to illustrate the collective strength inherent in the stories of volunteers, a treasure trove of experiences deserving to be shared and celebrated.

There's a memory that keeps resurfacing for me that I feel is relevant to this call for storytelling. For a period in the late 2000s to 2010, my father and I were involved in a project with Conservation Volunteers Australia. For one particular trip, we were loaded into a Toyota Hilux modified to carry people in the back and taken on a day excursion to Ravenswood, a small gold mining town in the Charters Towers Region, loosely bounded by the Flinders Highway to the northwest.

Ravenswood has a rich history, much of which would go unnoticed if not for the word of mouth passed among North Queenslanders. While there, we were given a tour of the London Mine and the heritage-listed Ravenswood Courthouse and Police Station. Now a museum nestled among the apples and rubber vines on the northern corner of Macrossan and Raven Streets, the site comprises three buildings erected in 1882: the courthouse, the police station, and the holding cells. Overlooking the Elphinstone Creek, these structures were removed in 1965 and later returned to the site during the 1980s.

As we explored each of the single storey timber buildings under their corrugated iron rooves and along the nice wooden verandas, my youthful eyes saw a cardboard box, the kind usually used for document storage, on the veranda porch. Without a lid, I saw it was loaded with books. They showed various signs of age, such as worn covers and traces of where silverfish clearly chewed through.

Peering at the books, I noticed titles hinting at possible themes of history, crime thrillers, rural tales, romance and maybe more. I felt a strong mix of emotions. On one hand, it was heartening to see these books had survived the years. But on the other, there was something melancholic about their resting place. Here, in a museum in a quiet town on a vast continent, showing signs of neglect. Would anyone read them now? Would anyone be curious enough to pick them up, to make time for their stories? Was this all that remained of their authors' legacy?

And then I wondered: if I became published, would my own works one day end up here too? Would that be an honour, or a sorrowful sight?

I still wonder that... To have my work gather dust in a box on a museum porch. Maybe it's both those things. But what I do know is that stories, even forgotten ones, have a strange way of echoing through time. And if someone, one day, stumbles across my words and feels even a flicker of what I felt looking into that box, then maybe that's enough. Or perhaps they find it in a street library, old shop, or on an old shelf in a rural property. That last one was a major book haul for me personally.

Maybe that's the quiet legacy we all leave behind.

To that end, my good friend, fellow author, and past mentor of mine, Rebeccah Statham, once said a phrase during an Instagram livestream that has stuck with me: *"Don't die with the fire still inside of you."* It gave me such pause with its resonance and would continue popping up from time to time.

Her book, *Ignite Your Spark*, which I beta read in quiet solitude while walking across Yarrawonga Drive, was all about finding your inner vision and showing it to the world, and then some. That book is what inspired me to seek becoming published.

Over time, I would lose some good friends and family. Some passed, satisfied at the end of a good long life, while others were gone abruptly, and I'll always think that those were too soon, for they could have offered just a little more to share.

All I know is that I wanted to bring my own fire out. Find the spark that would burn bright. That's what I tell myself when I'm feeling low with writer's block, self-doubt, or far sight lost.

Now, when I sit down to write, whether it's in the comfort of my house or on a peaceful trip, I think of all the sparks I've seen. Some still burning in others. Some left behind. But my own fire? It's no longer a flicker waiting to be lit. It dances on the page, however imperfectly. I've made peace with not knowing how long it will burn, only that I must keep feeding it, and sharing its light while I can.

This is my story, in our story...

Chapter Three

Papua New Guinea Part I – Milne Bay and Oro Bay

My trajectory towards volunteering was charted long before the events of the Townsville Floods came to pass. During my first tenure at Central Queensland University, an opportunity to explore the world a little further presented itself. I had previously travelled with family considerably, from the bustling streets of Japan to Indonesia and the Chiang Rai Province of Thailand.

Yet, it was the unforgettable expedition through the cultural tapestry of Turkey, the azure waters of the Aegean Sea, and the historic realms of Greece in 2015 that left their indelible mark. In August, the 100th anniversary of the second wave, my family and I made a pilgrimage to Gallipoli in honour of my great-grandfather, James Daniel Byrne, a man whose legacy continues to this day.

Jim Byrne was a man of integrity. Honest to a fault, respectfully outspoken, loyal, and possessed of both strength and a rare kindness. He had a dry wit and an exceptional gift for storytelling, often surrounded by true friends drawn to his quiet wisdom and generosity. He gave freely of his time and always stood by those he cared about.

For him, truth was non-negotiable. My Aunt Yvonne, his daughter, once told me how she was chided for misdemeanours, punished for lies. He taught her and others that it was better to break a rule and own up than to lie your way out of it. That ideal has stayed with her throughout life, and she doubted I'd ever told a lie. In many ways, this deeply ingrained moral compass has guided me through my professional life just as much as my personal one.

Jim had no time for bludgers or those looking for handouts. Despite being gassed in France, shot in the leg, and left with shrapnel embedded in his body, he refused to claim a military pension. When he was terminally ill in 1968, hospital staff were shocked to learn that, as a World War I veteran, he received no government support. They began the process of getting him the pension he so rightfully deserved, but he passed away before it was approved. His death left his widow without financial support, a consequence of his stubborn pride and his refusal to accept anything he felt he hadn't earned.

He once told Aunt Yvonne that when the war ended in 1918, soldiers were given two options: sign a quick medical clearance and go straight home, or line up and go through a thorough assessment, the infamous "hoops." Though he had been hospitalised in England, severely injured, and clearly in need of further care, he chose the fastest route home. To him, the war was over, and that was all that mattered.

Jim also had a larrikin's sense of humour. He rose to the rank of corporal, though he often joked that he "could've been a zebra" for all the stripes he earned and lost during his service. He was a man who could take the world seriously but never took himself too seriously.

In the 1950s, when Catholic traditions were followed with rigidity, the practice of Adoration of the Blessed Eucharist was a profound expression of faith. It lasted 24 hours, with someone always present in the church, praying. The men of the parish often took the night shifts, and true to his character, Jim Byrne volunteered for the 2am slot, committing to two hours of quiet devotion.

One particular night, Jim's dedication went beyond expectation. When his family woke up that morning, he still wasn't home. He finally walked in around 7:30am, explaining that no one had come to relieve him, so he stayed until the priest arrived for the 6am. For Jim, it wasn't a question of obligation but of responsibility. In his mind, "if something has to be done, it is done."

Jim had a pragmatic view of war, stripped of any illusion of glory. He carried the weight of his memories he never shared and avoided the mateship of the RSL. For him, Anzac Day was not a celebration but a solemn observance. The day began at church, followed by the parade. Yet, Jim never marched. Instead, he stood silently, watching others as they marched, offering them his quiet and steadfast respect.

And respect, both given and earned, was perhaps the cornerstone of Jim Byrne's philosophy. It shaped his actions, his relationships, and his legacy. Whether it was staying through the night in an empty church or honouring his fellow servicemen without fanfare, Jim exemplified a life guided by an unshakable sense of duty, humility, and reverence.

Aunt Yvonne has told me several times there's a lot of Jim in myself.

Another odyssey stood out as particularly relevant to my narrative of the Townsville Floods, the uncharted terrain of Papua New Guinea.

The lead up to this can be traced back to 2011, during my Year 9 of high school. That was an interesting year, but amidst the teenage angst and high school banter about funny viral YouTube videos, I was also engaged in the YWAM Youth Street program. I became a fervent participant in various dance teams, forging some connections that transcended time, and others that remain with the book ends of that phase of life. The friendships cultivated during those dance-filled endeavours became an enduring testament and laid the groundwork for my subsequent involvement in the community.

Then in 2016, my father, John Byrne, became interested in the Medical Ship. Although he is a lawyer most of the day, my dad was always a sailor at heart. You could see it in the house. Nautical portraits on the walls, weathered memorabilia from past races, from the Sydney-Hobart Yacht Race to Hong Kong-Manila and Cairns-Samarai Island. His wardrobe always hinted at it too: polos with yacht club insignias, boat shoes worn smooth, and caps from regattas gone by. His ties to the sea run deep, as do his friendships forged on deck. He played a major role in the Townsville Sailing Club for many years, not just as a member, but as a mentor, leader, and organiser.

Sailing wasn't just a hobby. In 1986, he was a key team member in the crew that won the World 12-Metre Yacht Racing Championship. That success earned him a coveted spot on the Australian team for the 1987 America's Cup, the most prestigious sailing race in the world. In a field dominated by lifelong athletes, my father, a lawyer from Townsville, stood out. Not because he was the fastest or the strongest, but because of his heart, discipline, and refusal to give up.

He demonstrated a fierce commitment to the team. As Greg Barnes, the crew's fitness instructor, recalled, my father would knock on his door at 5:30am sharp if his light wasn't on, making sure no one was late for training. Barnes himself admitted in his memoir that during the first training program, he didn't expect my dad to last. He nearly threw up during the warmup exercise, not even the hard drills, and yet, he kept coming back. Despite applying for the physically demanding role of mastman, a job requiring not only strength but elite conditioning, he was undeterred. There was something in him that caught Barnes' eye: a kind of mental tenacity that couldn't be taught.

As a mastman, he was the vital link between the foredeck and the aftdeck, responsible for synchronising the movements of the entire crew. That role requires not just skill, but a sense of situational awareness and timing that you can't teach. For my dad, that kind of teamwork wasn't just learned. It was instinctive. He didn't think about it as something special. It was just the way you work.

That's the thing about my dad. If something matters to him, he will give it everything he has. That attitude hasn't changed with age. He speaks with a deep, immaculate voice like those that dominate his generation. Whenever I travel with him, whether it's for volunteer work, sailing trips, or just day-to-day errands, I feel ten feet tall and bulletproof beside him.

Getting ready for this trip was an adventure in its own right. One thing we did was get our immune systems ready. Immunisations from malaria, cholera and hepatitis were taken. Eventually, all the paperwork and preparations were complete. We were ready to set off...

As the holiday season brought 2016 to a close, I would volunteer for Stable on the Strand – a local nativity event sponsored by YWAM. While I was walking around as one of the Three Wise Men and writing people's names in Ancient Greek as the Scribe, I would meet with the various DTS (Discipleship Training School) volunteers, having come to Townsville from all over the world, mostly Europe and the United States, following their own paths. I would work closer with them during the event's bump out. That night was a long one of carrying loads, deconstructing displays, wrapping up wiring and more. The humid summer air persisted into midnight, even the sea breeze had to compete with it. Despite the challenges, we all persisted in good spirit. Finally, the work was done by one in the morning.

Little did I know at the time that we would meet again, under similar circumstances.

The year ticked over to 2017, and the days ahead would be in anticipation of Papua New Guinea. Said days were usually walking to and from the gym, under dark overcast skies and over rain-soaked road, listening to Ernest Hemingway's *The Old Man And The Sea*, which I thought was an appropriate pick for the future sea trip. On the 7th of January, my father and I practiced piloting and manoeuvring one of the Sailing Club's RHIB motorboats. We would be using those a lot on the Medical Ship later on. Fittingly enough, it was grey overcast with light rain that day too, which added to the practice.

Finally, it was the morning of 16 January 2017. My father and I waited for the QantasLink airliner that would take us from Townsville to Cairns. It was a new day in every sense. In the waiting area, I could see some people in YWAM uniforms and fellow volunteers – My shipmates for the next few weeks.

As the plane taxied down the runway, I glanced out the window and watched as the familiar landscape of Townsville slowly gave way to the vast expanse of the sky. The thrill of being airborne filled me with a sense of freedom and possibility. During the flight, I marvelled at the breathtaking views from above. The coastline stretched out before us, its turquoise waters contrasting with the lush greenery of the surrounding landscapes.

During my travels in Papua New Guinea, I had a trusty companion with me in the form of a book called *Winter Hawk*. This thrilling novel, written by Craig Thomas, had captured my attention even before my journey began. As a reader of Thomas' previous works, I was eager to delve into the gripping storyline that I had searched for. *Winter Hawk*, published in 1987, continued the adventures of the protagonist, Mitchell Gant, who had previously been introduced in the *Firefox* novels as was played by Clint Eastwood in the movie. In this particular instalment, Gant embarks on a daring mission to prevent the launch of a Soviet space shuttle at Baikonur. The stakes are high, with the operation taking place just before the signing of a crucial arms reduction treaty.

The book, a large hardcover edition, was a possession that I had sought out specifically for my journey. Its pages were filled with fast-paced action and suspense, keeping me captivated during my downtime as I explored the wonders of Papua New Guinea. Back in the dorm, I would often find myself immersed in the world of *Winter Hawk*, escaping into the thrilling mission of Mitchell Gant, who piloted the MiG-31 Firefox prototype fighter aircraft in the eponymous novel. As I ventured through Papua New Guinea, my trusty copy of *Winter Hawk* served as both entertainment and inspiration.

Eventually, Port Moresby came into view. The capital city stood on the shores of a gulf on the south-western coast of the Papuan Peninsula. In its genesis, Port Moresby arose as a trade centre in the second half of the 19th century. Its moment in history came during World War II when it was a prime objective for conquest by the Imperial Japanese forces that failed to reach it in the end. Decades later, Port Moresby found itself in another world spotlight as it hosted the 2018 APEC Summit; an event that proved one of many in political events across the Pacific later on.

The moment I stepped onto the solid asphalt of the Papua New Guinea airport, a sense of accomplishment and anticipation washed over me. It had taken six years, but I had finally made it.

The airport terminal itself was a tribute to the unique Melanesian culture that defined Papua New Guinea. Its eccentric architecture, a blend of artistic design and traditional structural elements, reflected the heritage of the Papuan people. Everywhere I looked there were displays of traditional artwork, vividly showcasing the diverse and vibrant history of the countless tribes that had come together to form one united nation. In the distance, a mountain stood tall bearing the Hollywood-style letters "SKYVIEW."

As I cast my gaze toward the parking lot, a feeling of both excitement and caution surged within me. It was clear that I had reached my destination, but the sight of a Toyota vehicle loaded with riot gear, barred windows, and equipment straight out of a post-apocalyptic movie gave me pause. It was a stark reminder that Papua New Guinea, while captivating and beautiful, was not without its challenges. I had finally made it, I thought, and then I hoped I would make it out of there.

Our next flight awaited us, and I had the opportunity to catch a glimpse of a PNG Air aircraft along the way. This time, we boarded an Air Niugini Fokker 100 for our onward journey. I never imagined I'd be flying in one of those. The sky above was a mosaic of clouds and overcast conditions, painting a different picture from the clear skies I had experienced on my arrival. It was a subtle reminder that in Papua New Guinea, nature's beauty and unpredictability often danced hand in hand, promising a journey filled with both wonder and uncertainty.

Upon landing at Gurney Airport, formerly known as the No. 1 Strip, I was greeted by a small terminal nestled amidst lush green grass. As someone who visits Far North Queensland often, I am no stranger to tropical rainforests. Still, the sight of the vast mountainous landscape ahead filled me with a sense of awe and anticipation I had not felt before.

At the entrance of the airport, there stood an anti-aircraft gun, a reminder of the historical significance of this place. It served as a tribute to Squadron Leader C. R. "Bob" Gurney AFC, the Commanding Officer of No. 33 Squadron. Born in Corowa, Bob Gurney was a pioneering aviator in Papua New Guinea who began his flying career with Guinea Airways in 1929, eventually becoming its chief pilot. In 1936, he joined Qantas Empire Airways, piloting Empire flying boats and later went on to serve in the Royal Australian Air Force from March 1942. Gurney's memorial, featuring a three-bladed propeller, bore a poignant quote...

"A pioneer is one who goes before to prepare the way for those who follow."

After disembarking the aircraft, we were led into a small room, while a forklift transported our baggage into the receiving area. From there, we awaited our transport to Alotau in the warm humidity. Nearby was some kind of store for the local telecommunications company, Digicel, inviting people to "top up here," which was also decked out in Coco-Cola adverts for some reason.

Our ride then arrived. We all boarded the back of a truck on wooden seats that would not have looked out of place in a developing country's military. On the bumpy road, we watched as it took us on a road going through seemingly endless jungle and agriculture. Palm trees, mountains and the occasional house were the view. Eventually, more buildings came in sight such as the Alotau Supermarket. Then came a variety of fishing boats docked in a small bay. People and a variety of cars were roaming the street.

The lengthy drive ended at the port, where the flag of Papua New Guinea waved with one of Milne Bay Province. Various items and vehicles were scattered across the facilities. Then we saw the boat, nestled at the dock and stationary like a sleeping giant. The MV YWAM PNG was a marvellous sight indeed. Four levels of decks reached into the sky, displaying the proud sponsors that kept the ship going.

Beyond were the lights of Alotau in the wider bay which glowed in the sunset over the water. As the various European and North American accents were heard amongst the crowd gathering for dinner, I saw the beautiful sunset over Milne Bay, with the sun dipping below the horizon. The sky was painted in a spectrum of colours, ranging from deep blues and purples to warm oranges and yellows. A stunning reflection on the calm waters of the bay resembling a golden staircase. The clouds in the sky added texture and depth to the scene, with some areas illuminated by the sun's last light while others remain in shadow. The overall effect was serene and breathtaking, highlighting the natural beauty of Milne Bay during sunset.

As I sat down to eat, I saw that many of these people were of the DTS that I remember seeing from the previous year's Stable on the Strand. I hardly thought I'd work with them again, much less in this part of the world. Some of these people included a Portuguese girl with round glasses, a Welshman who would be a mate of mine in the deck crew, a blonde girl from Tennessee, a Chilean man, and a lot more.

After dinner, I was introduced to my first job as deck crew: Gangway watch! I would sit on a chair overlooking, you guessed it, the ship's gangway connecting her starboard side to the concrete platform. I would record people coming and going with a board of all our shipmates' names. The rest of the time, I'd sit there, pacing around, listening to music or watching videos like *Top Gear* episodes. A woman that would sometimes have the shift before played solitaire on her phone, saying it's a game against yourself.

One surprising moment came when some of the young adults on the YWAM DTS came in, and they told me they were going to prank one of their own. One young lad was brought out onto the gangway, and after a few seconds, a bucketload of water fell on him from the upper level. Splash! They got him good, and he took it in good spirit, whooping and cheering with them... and then one of the ship's crew arrived on the scene, quietly telling him the children on board were trying to sleep.

That's another thing. There were kids along for this outreach. I was surprised to see quite a few of them. In particular, there were children of the Hoover family with their mother and father. One of our senior crew brought his family along too. My father was also surprised, because bringing a family along is a luxury in the shipping world. That was one of a few lucky breaks this ship offered – a piece of home in uncharted, treacherous waters.

As the still night descended and progressed, my father and I were introduced to my senior officer, Toby White, who was a no-nonsense, tough-as-nails ex-merchantman, with the "ex" part being debatable. Dad even advised me that this guy seemed to be such.

The next morning, I was woken from our room in "the dungeon," and was on gangway watch again. The sun rose over my station, casting a soft, golden glow across the scene. The silhouette of palm trees, buildings, and a crane or port structure was visible against the backdrop of the sky which was gradually lightening from deep shades of blue to lighter hues. A lone cloud was illuminated by the rising sun, adding a dramatic effect to the scene. The overall atmosphere was calm and peaceful, highlighting the quiet beauty of Alotau in the early morning hours. The water was so still and calm you could see faint traces of coral underneath the docks. The town of Alotau came into morning once more, and the misty mountains that encircled the bay were an incredible sight.

From there, the day began. After breakfast, we were all introduced to our various roles of deck crew. The captain of the ship was Jan

Alnes, formerly Royal Norwegian Navy. One of my first duties was helping him install a new railing on one of the ship decks. There was a great deal of ruined screws, which were immediately discarded. The morning heat was staggering at the time, even in the shade.

Yet even that competed with Toby's hot temper. For someone aboard a missionary ship, Toby had quite the mouth, but if anyone wanted to address it, they would be braver than the rest of us. I personally didn't care, and I don't think any of the crew did either. Come to think of it, the crew was perhaps the least religious part of the ship. According to my father, they gathered up at the end of the day in the bridge and let off some steam, not that I blame them. They had some of the toughest duties on the ship, after all. As day progressed, we began training in our various roles as the deck crew. Some of our duties included maintenance, cleanliness, and operating various equipment. It was hard work for a new person like me, and it became quite clear that I was the least experienced of the team. I knew I had to toe the line and get in quick for teams are only as strong as the weakest link, and I did not intend to be that for long.

However, as the saying goes, the harder the battle, the sweeter the victory, for the day yielded a sunset that was even greater than yesterday. As it arrived in a small parting between the mountains and the cloud, the rays of sun erupted in an explosion of orange glow. A lining beam of light sparkled in the water, cascading all the way up to the sun in the golden staircase again. It coloured the sky in various shades of gold and dark greyish blue, amongst the various swirling clouds of the humid air. It was truly a remarkable sight, unique to this area, that I would never forget. Every angle was a new image, another portrait of the uncharted tropics. On the top deck, I saw the various couples aboard the ship indulging in it, marvelling in English, German, and Latin Spanish.

To my left, a small but vivid emblem of Papua New Guinea fluttered in the breeze, capturing my attention with its captivating design. The flag was a symphony of symbolism, divided diagonally from the upper hoist-side corner to the lower fly-side corner. In the black hoist, the familiar white Southern Cross adorned the field with its four larger five-pointed stars and the smaller star, a celestial homage to the Southern Hemisphere's night sky. Soaring majestically in the red fly was the golden silhouette of a Raggiana bird-of-paradise. The harmonious interplay between the black hoist and the red fly showcased the traditional colours of numerous Papua New Guinean tribes, weaving a tapestry of cultural diversity.

Against the backdrop of the breeze, the fluttering flag and symbols like it encapsulated the essence of Papua New Guinea's heritage and the collective identity of its people. Even the Coke cans had unique tribal art just below the rim, as I took a picture of later that night. That was in our room, comprised of a double bunk, a work desk, a small bathroom, a porthole and a map of Papua New Guinea on the wall.

After a rather short sleep, I made my way through the hall of our sleeping quarters in the lower deck. A maritime tradition, or trend at least, was that the officer's cabins were on the lower deck. We were crewmen, not officers. While these may or may not have been at least a little more spacious, they did provide us occupants with some privacy. Ventilated air and no natural light filtered down, but it was a huge improvement over the generally cramped, dark and airless conditions of ships of old. Unlocking the door's latch, I took my position at gangway watch. My father had offered to extend his shift until 5:30AM so I could sleep in a little more, and while I was grateful, it was still a big ask of my young self. Nevertheless, I sat there, listening to instrumental folk music that I had stored on my phone when the sun's rays came over the horizon once more, engulfing the bay in a ginger shine.

The morning saw another ship move past, and locals in our crew whistled out to them. It was more of the usual duties and becoming accustomed to them. The sunset was a bright white glow that disappeared behind the clouds as rain began closing in. The blissful laughter and light-hearted conversation of the youthful missionaries filled the deck. I was glad to see the usual indulgence in the younger years, seen usually when the shadows leave in the night. Together, throughout this outreach, they would come face to face with the challenges, learn lessons through them and make memories that would never fade. I certainly did. Then the night came, and stillness came once more.

The next day, we were finally allowed to explore the shore. My father and I checked out of the port and made our way through the hot sunny air toward the town of Alotau.

On the shore strand stood a prominent tall, dark stone monument inscribed with *"Battle of Milne Bay 1942."* The monument is situated on a circular platform surrounded by four flagpoles. The memorial overlooked the calm body of water that was Milne Bay itself, with lush green grass and small shrubs. A dramatic sky filled with dark, stormy clouds added a solemn and reflective atmosphere to the scene. In the distance, there were mountains partially obscured by the clouds, providing a picturesque yet sombre setting that honoured the memory of the battle and its significance in history. It served as a solemn reminder of the bravery and sacrifice displayed by the Australians, Papua New Guineans, and their allies during the intense fighting that took place in 1942. A quote from Ivan Southall's book, *Bluey Truscott,* around the memorial detailed how *"the sweating jungle crowded in upon it and mist sat on the densely scrubbed mountains and the very air sweated."*

Back in the day, as the Pacific War was raging, the threat to Milne Bay developed rapidly. Japanese aircraft carried out reconnaissance missions and bombed the base that is now Gurney Airport several times. On the 24th of August, an American bomber crew spotted an invasion fleet, and the worst was yet to come. Standing in their way was an inexperienced militia and the 18th Brigade that had seen action in North Africa as part of the Australian Imperial Force. Despite Australian and American aircraft attacking the enemy fleet, the Japanese landed troops on the northwestern side of Milne Bay near Ahioma before dawn on the 26th. As recalled by Lieutenant Colonel Alex Meldrum, his 61st Battalion that was facing the initial attack in darkness was hopelessly outnumbered and outflanked, so they started to fall back, but on every possible occasion they turned and fought savagely.

As the arduous days rolled by, the Japanese landed tanks and troops at Milne Bay. The Australian troops kept fighting them, but without infantry anti-tank weapons and outnumbered still, they continued to be pushed back. The base area and airstrips continued to be bombed, while the hard-pressed militiamen were reinforced by infantry and artillery gunners. Over the next two days and nights, fighting in the jungle was hard and costly. Heavy rain and poor communications confused the situation. Master Sergeant Jules Archer of the US Army Signal Corps captured the atmosphere with his words: "*To the sweating, exhausted diggers, each new day seemed beyond endurance, yet they continued to endure and fight without complaint.*"

Field Marshal Sir William Slim, the British commander in Burma at the time, later remarked, "*In August and September 1942, Australian troops had at Milne Bay in New Guinea, inflicted on the Japanese that first undoubted defeat on land. If the Australians had done it... so could we.*" His words underscored the significance of this victory, as it marked the first definitive defeat of the Japanese on land during the war. Major-General Cyril Clowes, commander of the Milne Force, also praised the efforts of the RAAF, stating, "*I wish to place on record my appreciation of the magnificent efforts on the part of our RAAF comrades. The success of the operation was in great measure due to their untiring and courageous work."*

The battle also saw acts of individual heroism such as that of Corporal John French, VC, of the 2/9th Battalion, who tragically lost his life at 28 years old while throwing grenades to silence two enemy machine gun posts. His fiancée poignantly remarked on hearing of his passing, *"We don't know the worth of quiet boys until they are called upon to do something big,"* reflecting the bravery and sacrifice of the soldiers. Another notable figure was Maiogura, a Milne Bay nurse awarded the Medal of Loyal Service, who humbly said, *"I give thanks to God that I was able, in some small measure, to assist my very good Australian friends."*

Private Bill Spencer of the 2/9th Battalion described how, following the battle, *"additional forces were moving in building a base on the southern side of the bay... installing workshops for a major maintenance to allied naval vessels. The airships were extended on the northern shore, and Milne Bay became a major base."*

These original quoted sayings, preserved within the context of the Battle of Milne Bay, capture the extraordinary circumstances and the indomitable spirit of those who fought in the face of adversity. They serve as poignant reminders of the valour, resilience, and mateship displayed by the individuals involved, ensuring that their memory and contributions are forever honoured.

After that, we began exploring the town a little bit more. There was the area near the marketplace where a few people walked along a dirt path which had several puddles and patches of wet ground from the recent rain. The path led to the waterfront where various boats were moored. The boats were small to medium-sized; some covered with tarps and others with supplies and equipment on their decks. The waterfront area was active with people engaged in different activities, possibly preparing for or returning from a journey. A group of people could be seen gathered under the shelter that was the marketplace. Further away was lush, green vegetation, and dense trees lining the shore. Then came a huge assortment of sugar canes, palm trees and various other trees near a plantation, and a sign that thanked us for visiting Alotau.

Along the other side of the road was a lush, green landscape in a more rural area of Alotau. The foreground was dominated by tall grasses and dense vegetation which extended into a thick jungle in the background. The jungle featured a variety of trees, including palm trees and other tropical flora, creating a rich and vibrant environment. Amidst the dense greenery, a few structures were partially visible, indicating human habitation. These buildings were scattered throughout the landscape, blending into the natural surroundings. The sky above was overcast, with a blanket of clouds suggesting a calm yet possibly rainy day.

Once again, the sun was setting over the horizon. This time it was surrounded by dark grey cloud which caught its light and shaded it as well. Eventually the grey dark wall of rain and a heavy cloud came across from the right of the view, like a curtain to end the day.

During my watch shift that night, guarding the gangway, I noticed something. I would not notice it again until I saw the photo I took of it in the corner of my eye when exploring the various photos over time. It was a yellow vest hanging on the whiteboard that was displaying our instructions. This high-visibility vest had a specific wording written in marker: *"I 1 2 Live YWAM."* Upon reading it aloud, I realised that it was a play on "I Want To Live." That phrase called back memories of Youth Street in 2012. That was the catch phrase that had a variety of meanings, chief among them was a cry of support to affected children which our charitable actions aimed to help. I remember it was the main motto of the Saxby family's actions in Cambodia, rescuing trafficked girls. There was a girl named Paulien in particular who I was a close friend of in those days. We went our separate ways, but my promises were kept, nonetheless. How it ended up here spoke of a few possibilities. Perhaps a previous wearer was affiliated with that charity initiative, or it was written on by a higher authority. That one wording on the vest confirmed to me that I was here on their behalf, fulfilling a promise I made to step up to the plate and volunteer.

The next day, after our usual duties, I read the January / February 2017 issue of the *Aero Australia* magazine that I had brought with me. I do miss this magazine, though *Wings* magazine has filled that void. I have many of its copies still in my possession from before it folded shortly after its amazing coverage of the Avalon Airshow in 2019. One article, nestled within its Historic Aviation segment, cast a spotlight on the illustrious history of the Curtiss P-40 Kittyhawk in Australian service. This remarkable aircraft of the Royal Australian Air Force played pivotal roles in historic battles, including those in Milne Bay, Port Moresby, and New Guinea. Reading about these battles at the very sites they unfolded was a poignant connection to the past to me. A captivating photograph featured Squadron Leader Keith "Bluey" Truscott in P-40E Kittyhawk A29-142 during the pivotal Battle of Milne Bay. Additional photos showcased P-40Ns of 84 Squadron in Ross River, Townsville in June 1945, mere months before the war's conclusion.

The pages also unfolded an artistic depiction of Kittyhawk A29-153/0 of 75 Squadron RAAF, illustrating the strategic overpainting of the US Army Air Force fuselage star and the subsequent application of the RAAF roundel. A particularly intriguing image captured a moment of field maintenance in New Guinea, with

A TIME FOR VOLUNTEERS 55

the crew diligently changing the propeller of 76 Squadron's P-40M A29-323 against the backdrop of palm trees.

In a remarkable twist of coincidence, another article detailed *"The Odyssey of 77 Squadron RAAF,"* which also played a role in the historic theatre of Milne Bay in New Guinea. As Japanese forces launched a major air raid on Milne Bay, the valiant efforts of 75 and 77 Squadrons intercepted the onslaught, resulting in the downing of four bombers and two fighters, with an additional five likely bombers. The stories embedded in those pages served as a powerful reminder of the courage and sacrifices made by those who served, soaring through the skies over New Guinea during a pivotal chapter in history.

As I immersed myself in the tales of historic aviation within the pages of the *Aero Australia* magazine, a remarkable parallel unfolded, linking the resilient spirit of those who served in the skies over New Guinea to the ethos of volunteering and the challenges of hard tropical work. Much like the dedicated crews depicted in the field maintenance photo amidst palm trees, volunteers in tropical regions face their own battles against the elements, working tirelessly to maintain and uplift communities. The stories of the Curtiss P-40 Kittyhawk, a steadfast workhorse during pivotal battles, resonated with the enduring commitment embodied by volunteers facing the challenges of a tropical landscape. The magazine's coverage of squadrons intercepting air raids over Milne Bay highlighted the courage and collaboration required in the face of adversity, a reflection of the mateship and shared purpose that defines the efforts of volunteers. These narratives underscored the timeless themes of resilience, sacrifice, and collective endeavour, weaving a narrative drapery that seamlessly connects the historic skies of New Guinea to the modern-day challenges embraced by those dedicated to the hard tropical work of volunteering.

This historical tour into the volunteering and service of the past continued the next day when we went a further distance to another memorial site. It was a well-maintained field of grass and gardens with a mountain visible far beyond the tree line. A plaque was standing on the eastern side of what was in 1942 the No. 3 airstrip, later named Turnbull Field, in honour of Squadron Leader Peter St. George Turnbull DFC, the commanding officer of No. 76 squadron who lost his life during a strafing run on Japanese positions near Sanderson's Bay on the 27th of August 1942. His squadron's motto was *"To strive, to seek, to find, not to yield."* A memorial was erected to the 61st Australian Battalion, the Queensland Cameron Highlanders, who paid the supreme sacrifice during the Battle of Milne Bay. It was here at this point on the 28th of August 1942 that the 7th and 18th Brigades, assisted by units of the RAAF in the United States Army, stopped the Japanese force that was advancing towards the airfields.

The cenotaph explained further development of the local area after the war. The purchasing of the Cameron Plateau above Sanderson's Bay in 1961 meant that in following years, government offices were relocated to the plateau on the site of the wartime American Hospital. In 1967, the town was named "Alotau," meaning "Peaceful Bay" in the local Suau dialect. By 1976, when Papua New Guinea gained independence, Alotau was well established as the provincial capital in the Alotau Urban LLG (Local-Level Government area). The people of Milne Bay look forward to a bright future but will always remember the events of 1942 that helped shape the area.

This excursion, I may say, underscored the enduring theme of serving a greater cause. The cenotaph narrated the post-war transformation of the local area, symbolising the resilience and regeneration that follows even the darkest times.

As a side note, while we were waiting for the bus to take us back to the port, Dad found himself engaging in conversation with a local man. He pointed out that this province is not connected to the capital via highway, only by air and sea. The local thought that it was better that Alotau was not connected to Port Moresby, for if it did, all the ugly urban infrastructure, in his view, would come to Alotau and it would not be as pretty.

After having lunch at the local café and shopping at the Alotau supermarket, we returned to the boat. As we approached the port, the sight of the unique flags flying caught our attention. The flag of Papua New Guinea, with its vibrant colours and distinctive design, fluttered majestically in the breeze. Beneath it, the flag of Milne Bay Province, featuring a vertical green stripe in the leftmost section representing the lush greenery and rich natural resources of the region, a white stripe in the middle section, and right section diagonally divided into two triangles: the upper triangle is maroon with a yellow star, and the lower triangle is blue. Next to them, the flag of the PNG Ports Corporation, with its emblematic design, represented the vital role of the ports in the nation's commerce and connectivity. The display of these flags not only highlighted the local and national identity but also underscored the significance of the port as a hub of activity and a gateway to the broader region.

Culturally, the Milne Bay region is often referred to as the Massim, a term derived from Misima Island. Massim societies are typically characterized by matrilineal descent, elaborate mortuary rituals, and intricate systems of ritual exchange such as the Kula ring. The local culture varies significantly from one island group to another, and even between nearby islands.

By the end of the day, our time in Milne Bay ended, the ship's lines were let go, the engine rumbled, and the mighty vessel made her way into the twilight. Under a darkening sky with the evening star breaking through, she moved out to the bay. The view was dark, with only a few scattered lights illuminating the shoreline and distant buildings. The lights reflected in the water created a peaceful, almost mysterious ambiance. The rippling surface of the water added to the calm feeling, while the sparsely lit areas suggested a quiet, less urbanised environment. The glowing colours of the lights, mostly warm yellows and cooler greens, contrasted against the dark surroundings, emphasising the tranquillity of the coastal town at night.

High in the sky, deep shades of blue and black rose above the remnants of twilight near the horizon. Venus, the lone Evening Star, hung prominently in the darkening sky, like a symbol of the other celestial bodies in the endless world of space. Below, dark cloud formations lingered near the horizon, silhouetted against the fading light. The overall scene evoked a sense of calm and quiet beauty, perfect for reflection or peaceful observation of the natural world.

The rays of light from the town and the port shrank as they became further away. Eventually, darkness descended entirely. I retired to my bunk, illuminated by a fluorescent light on the wall it was against. My pyjama shirt was one from the supermarket that read *"I Love Milne Bay,"* but instead of where the red heart would be, it was a red bird-of-paradise. The engine hummed in the background as I fell asleep, getting some rest before the real volunteering work began.

The following morning found the ship still in motion, and peering out of my room's porthole revealed a captivating sight of the deep blue sea racing past. Stepping outside, I was met by the expansive view of a lush, elevated coastline stretching along the horizon. The ship was navigating its course towards what appeared to be a small settlement nestled in a cove: This was Oro Bay, within the larger Dyke Ackland Bay.

Situated in the Oro (Northern) Province of Papua New Guinea, the small settlement was approximately twenty-four kilometres southeast of Buna. Notably, it played a crucial role as a staging area and terminus for convoys of Operation Lilliput, particularly during the pivotal Battle of Buna-Gona and subsequent operations. An advanced base established by the United States at Oro Bay boasted a liberty ship wharf at the bay's southern end, shore installations, and strategically positioned anti-aircraft gun batteries in the surrounding hills. The historical significance of Oro Bay reached its peak on 28 March 1943 when Imperial Japanese planes launched an attack on shipping and harbor facilities, resulting in the sinking of SS *Masaya* and SS *Bantam*. Adjacent to this, Oro Bay Airfield played a pivotal role during that era, serving as a strategic location for military operations.

Such were the more commonly known details of Oro Bay, but delving further into its depths would reveal intricacies known only to those fortunate enough to set foot there. As we approached the bay, the details came into sharper focus, offering a firsthand perspective that transcended mere descriptions. The designated port, operated by PNG Ports Corporation Limited, gradually unfolded before us with its limited wharf facilities. To its left, shipping crates lined the waterfront, almost reaching out to touch the lapping waves. On the right, imposing storage tanks punctuated the landscape, framing the central feature of our impending docking, the wharf standing ready to welcome the ship.

The significance of the bay's name extends beyond mere nomenclature, as "Oro" translates to "welcome" in the native Orokaiva language, spoken across two hundred villages around Popondetta and part of the Binandere family of the non-Austronesian dialects. This linguistic connection intertwines with synonymous elements of tapa, tattoos, the Tufi fjords (to be explored later), the world's largest butterfly known as Queen Alexandra's Birdwing, and the historic Kokoda Track, symbolising the province's moment in history during the intense New Guinea Campaign of the Pacific War.

These diverse facets contribute to the province's uniqueness and serve as a catalyst for its name change. This book will refer to the province by that name for simplicity's sake. Although the alteration lacks formal constitutional recognition, the term "Oro" has gained widespread usage, akin to the informal but once widely adopted "North Solomons Province" for Bougainville Province.

The culture of Oro is woven with unspoken traditions preserved and handed down through generations. This cultural legacy is seen as a guiding light, illuminating the identity of the Oro people and delineating the character, manners, values, and rituals that shape their daily lives and ceremonial practices. It stands as a source of a heritage that not only signifies their origins and ancestry but also encapsulates the essence of the entire province. The principal primary industry of this province is oil palm.

As the vessel neared her docking point, the mesmerising scene intensified. I remained on deck, captivated by the vibrant tableau unfurling before me. The lush greenery of palm trees and various other trees speckled the landscape beneath grassy hills, crowned by a communications tower reaching towards the heavens. The clouds seemed to graze the surface of the higher peaks beyond, creating a connection between earth and sky. In this moment, standing at the precipice of arrival, I couldn't help but marvel at the natural beauty that surrounded Oro Bay, a place where the known details blended seamlessly with the unspoken tales etched into its terrain.

Shortly thereafter, our volunteer duties took a crucial turn: Firefighter training. My shipmate, Rahul Sagar, and I were paired up for this task, a responsibility that many are well acquainted with. Our roles alternated between being the individual donning the firefighting gear, and the one tasked with applying it. The ensemble comprised sage fireproof overalls, yellow safety hats, and oxygen masks, though, for training purposes, the masks dispensed normal air rather than pure oxygen, a precautionary measure outside of actual emergencies. On either that day or the following, the entire ship engaged in a comprehensive fire drill, heralded by the resonating sound of the bell.

When the drill commenced and the bell echoed through the ship, we promptly executed our roles, swiftly donning our gear and navigating to the simulated location of the fire. The collective effort culminated in successfully extinguishing the imaginary blaze, a testament to the efficacy of our training. In those moments, the significance of our volunteer efforts, even in simulated scenarios, mirrored the preparedness required for real emergencies, emphasising the importance of collective training and quick, coordinated responses to ensure the safety and well-being of all on board.

Another excursion beckoned us beyond the confines of Oro Bay, and I joined two ladies, one of them the ship's freelance photographer, in venturing outside the wire fencing. I was taking my photography through the humidity-stained camera lens of a Nokia smartphone I would damage in seawater just a few days later. Our journey unfolded, weaving through diverse scenes that would etch themselves into our memories. Following a shopping expedition at a sizable warehouse, our path led us to a straw and tinfoil house, perched elegantly over a lagoon, and an adjacent petroleum storage station. As we progressed, the village emerged, extending a warm welcome in the form of a tidy path of smooth sand bordered by meticulously arranged lines of plants.

The residents, with genuine hospitality, greeted us warmly, their excitement evident at the sight of visitors from different corners of the globe. The ship's arrival, carrying individuals from myriad nations, painted a vibrant picture of a world vast and interconnected, a perspective quite different from our own. In the heart of Oro Bay, our collective volunteering efforts became evident as we engaged with the residents, sharing in their joy and contributing to the community spirit. It was a poignant reminder that, for these residents, our volunteering endeavours played a role in sustaining their happiness and preserving the treasures they held dear. Beyond the physical landscapes we traversed, the deeper connection forged through our efforts highlighted the universal language of compassion and solidarity that reaches the far corners of the world.

As the day drew to a close, I found myself once again on gangway watch duty, my shift extending from the tranquil afternoon into the evening. The night brought with it an unexpected deluge, a torrential downpour that surpassed the familiar rhythm of a typical summer shower. The raindrops, larger and more forceful, caught the rays of the massive light casting its glow over the port, transforming the scene into a captivating spectacle. Illuminated by frequent bursts of lightning, the entire area danced with ephemeral flashes. Amidst this, my father engaged in conversation with Gideon, one of the local crewmen who sported a scraggly beard and stocky build. With his soft-spoken yet sarcastic sense of humour, Gideon also had a knack for chipping away at a coconut with a machete. As the rain poured relentlessly, the chatter continued on the gangway, illuminated by the play of light and dark.

The following day unfolded with a sense of routine, marked by the familiar cadence of our usual duties. As the sun rose and cast its golden hues over the maritime landscape, we embarked on tasks that had become second nature during our volunteering endeavours. While the specifics of each duty may not stand out in elaborate detail, the collective efforts of the crew continued to weave our shared commitment to service. In the rhythm of routine, there was a quiet acknowledgment of the essential roles we played in contributing to the greater cause, making each seemingly ordinary day a meaningful thread in the larger narrative of our volunteering journey at sea.

The next morning brought a shift in the rhythm of our maritime volunteering endeavours, introducing an intriguing chapter as we prepared the smaller motorboats. These nimble vessels would serve as our conduits, ferrying volunteers across to other settlements nestled along the pristine shores. Clad in a life jacket, I found my place on the rubber side, diligently ensuring the safe embarkation of others and their supplies. With a vroom of the engine, we embarked on a journey across the clear, smooth waters, venturing outward to sea.

A short distance away, the container ship, *Oriental Hero,* lay anchored, a quiet giant with minimal activity, hinting at a likely cargo-free state with its elevated draft. Brett, skilfully navigating at the helm, traced the green shoreline for ten miles until we reached the tranquil shores of Pongani. A hidden village shrouded in forgotten historical significance, Pongani once served as a staging area for the American 126th and 128th Regiments, as well as the Australian 2/6th Independent Company during the Battle of Buna-Gona.

Today, it is a small village in another form entirely. Entering a small lagoon, I could see straw houses between the trees. This marked the commencement of our exploration into uncharted territory. Some of these houses were marvels of craftsmanship, fashioned with various woods and intricate weaving, akin to Queenslander-style architecture, complete with clotheslines, stairs, and multiple rooms overlooking tidy courtyards. As we approached, the villagers gathered around, extending a warm welcome to their village. Such a welcome immediately told a story of the profound connections forged through the maritime volunteering efforts that I was now part of.

With our mission accomplished and supplies dropped off, I had a brief stay at Pongani. After using visual aids to educate the children on healthy eating, I remember talking with two people by the white sands of the beach. There was a man with white hair and beard who spoke with a Washington State accent. The other was Morgan, a Papua New Guinean-Canadian girl who usually worked alongside us crew, bearing a fascinating life story.

Brett and I made our way back to the ship. Once back on board, I found myself with some free time, a rare luxury. I decided to make the most of it, heading straight for the computer, eager to learn more about the region we were currently in. I began researching the Salamaua-Lae campaign, a pivotal series of battles during World War II. It was surreal to think that the very land where our volunteering efforts were making an impact had once been the site of such intense conflict. As I scrolled through historical accounts and photographs, such as those of the Australian 9th Division landing east of Lae on 4 September 1943, I was transported back to the dense jungles and steep ridges of Papua New Guinea, imagining the hardships and bravery of the soldiers who had fought there. I read about the Allied forces' daring landings, the fierce jungle warfare, and the relentless struggle to gain control of Salamaua and Lae, strategic locations crucial to the Pacific Theatre. The more I learned, the more connected I felt to the history of the place. It was humbling to realise that, in our own small way, we were contributing to the ongoing story of this region, long after the guns had fallen silent.

As the afternoon descended, we returned to Pongani to pick up the missionaries who had dedicated their day there. My explorations within the village expanded, revealing a vibrant tableau of daily life, a flourishing garden, children engrossed in playful sports, and villagers earnestly engaging with volunteers within a community facility.

As the clouds low in the sky darkened to signal the day's end, the villagers congregated on the shore to bid us farewell. The scene was a poignant mosaic of diverse ages and roles, men and women spanning the spectrum from young to elderly, and a venerable village elder standing at the forefront. Their collective presence, waving goodbye, painted a picture of gratitude, and the shared sense of community and goodwill lingered in the air as our speedboat slowly navigated away from the shore. The echo of farewells and the vivid snapshots of village life became indelible memories which we would take back to our homes across the world.

Getting back to the ship, however, would not be so easy. There were signs in the water followed by signs in the wind...

Huge, menacing rain clouds gathered across the sky as soon as the boat went out to sea. It was clear that we would have to make haste if we were to escape the storm. That would prove a futile task just a few minutes out at sea. Soon the wind and water began to sing – first quite low, then loud, and at last with a massive symphony of power. The waves began to pick up, turning the already bumpy ride into one of constant rising up and slamming down. Then came the soaking rain, coming down in large droplets, and with nothing to shield ourselves from it, we just had to ride it out. Lightning began striking the sky high above, followed swiftly by booms of thunder. Judging by the small sound delay between the two, it was quite clear that we were in the middle of the storm. We all held on tight. I was grabbing the rope on the rubber side so hard it turned my hands white and numb. My body would continue feeling lighter and heavier with each bump on the waves that seemingly lasted forever. These waves would not gently carry us home to safety, as they would in various tunes I have heard over time, instead being nature's wrath in motion. It's a sensation you would not expect, but would scarcely forget, like a memory for all time.

Looking further outside, trying to prevent myself from becoming seasick by looking inside the boat, I swear I could still see the local fishermen rowing out at sea in wooden canoes. I was amazed that they were still out at sea, continuing their little excursions of trying to find fish, even in choppy waters. One has to wonder how they made it back home, but this being a usual summer here meant they had more than enough experience to do so.

I had somehow made my way to the front of the boat, still holding the rope with an iron grip. The lightning kept cracking the sky and the thunder booming for some very long minutes as we braved the Dyke Ackland Bay. There was no way around or above such a tremendous obstacle, only through. Enduring the huge waves, I made a promise to never complain about a summer back home. No matter how rough, hot or humid those would ever be, they were certainly not Papua New Guinea's summers. I joked to the girl next to me, somehow saying over the din that I'd tell people they wouldn't even know how much I could complain about the weather. I held true to that promise, for I don't voice complaints about rough weather.

I write about them instead.

Finally, after circling around more land, the *Oriental Hero* came into view, its lights a welcoming sight of civilisation after enduring the fury of the sea. We made it back to the bay and began circling around the ship to prepare to dock. Brett ordered me to the front of the boat. It was now up to me to latch the rope on, a task I struggled with in practice runs. A whole lot of responsibility had come onto my shoulders. Everyone was relying on me in the thick of a storm to get back onto the ship as soon as possible, even as the rain kept pounding and the waves churning. I grabbed the rope and tried to apply the latch, but it refused to open. I tried again and again, crushing my thumbs to make it move. Brett was starting to get impatient and frustrated as I struggled to pry the latch open, "Come on, James! Don't make me come over there!"

I made him come over there. On the verge of losing his cool, he grabbed the latch and put it on. We would later learn from the captain as he inspected it that the mechanism inside had indeed rusted. That still didn't prevent me from having to practice clipping and unclipping it five times first thing the next morning. My telling of it not moving was seen as just an excuse.

Regardless of that, the boat was successfully hooked up, craned and placed in the ship's flank. Everyone was loaded off, and we were quite drenched. I was saturated and exhausted from enduring the craziest storm I had ever been under. Now, however, it was all over. The day's mission had been accomplished, and I felt so relieved. This was peak volunteering work for me, and I felt great for doing that. This was definitely the kind of story that I would talk about but would never really fully show what it was like to be there. That was something only those who participated in would really know.

With that out of the way, I turned to Brett and said something along the lines of, "Well, that was a good job." I said that in such a way that it would acknowledge and congratulate him for braving such a fierce storm. He then told me, emotionlessly and to the point, about my duties tomorrow. He turned around and walked away without another word. With that, all of the sense and relief that I had just mentioned felt much smaller. For a rookie like me it may have been a big achievement, but to the others it was just another day...

That night, still shaken from the ride, I continued my research, this time focusing on the landing at Lae in September of 1943. The more I read, the more vivid the events of that day became in my mind. I learned how Australian and American forces had launched a coordinated assault on Lae, a key Japanese stronghold. The operation involved an amphibious landing from the sea, the first major one undertaken by the Australian Army since the Gallipoli Campaign, along with paratroopers dropped further inland to cut off enemy escape routes. The Japanese defenders, though formidable, were gradually overwhelmed by the sheer determination and strategy of the Allied forces. It marked a significant turning point in the New Guinea campaign as the Allies regained control over the Huon Peninsula.

I could almost imagine the scene through the photo of a US Army Air Force B-24 Liberator bomber flying over explosions on the Salamaua Peninsula on 13 August, or the one of 9th Division's LSTs completing their unloading. Reading the personal accounts of soldiers who had fought in the battle added a deeply human element to the strategy and military manoeuvres. Those who volunteered for such a defence fought under unimaginable conditions, shaping the fate of the region we were now trying to help. There was something about studying these moments of the past that made me feel like my own work, in a small way, was part of a much larger continuum, one that stretched across decades of hardship, perseverance, and hope.

The next morning was an earlier start than usual. The lights of the port were a gentle glowing sanctuary as dawn began breaking. The crescent moon was in the sky – A welcoming sight after the storm yesterday. The lesson I learned from that is even after the roughest storm, the sky always clears, and the morning always comes, even after the darkest nights. The harder the storm, the sweeter the aftermath.

The sun began rising after we made our way onto the wharf with shades of orange and yellow blending into the darkening blue sky. A prominent silhouette of trees and hills was visible in the distance, while the bay's calm water reflected the fading light. A tall light pole stood on the dock, adding a human-made element to the natural beauty. In the foreground, I saw the wharf extending over the water, and to the right, a building with a corrugated metal roof rested near the shore.

During the lull in our duties, I would stare at the sunrise, briefly thinking for the moment, as its golden rays made their way across the sky and over the wall of cloud out at sea. I knew that this morning sun would be rising over my home of Australia, casting the east coast in its light. My friends from Melbourne to Brisbane and Townsville would be waking up to start their day on their way to work. Perhaps in that very moment they were getting up, starting with the morning coffee and continuing their daily lives. I, meanwhile, was here in Papua New Guinea, a tropical land that was a close equivalent to the edge of the world, inhabited by a much smaller population and worked in by a select few. I vowed to meet my friends again that I was thinking about in that moment, and I would again eventually. That morning, however, I was going to focus on the mission at hand. The volunteering work. The labour that I had signed up for so that others may experience an equally blissful morning.

Above us at equal height with the top of the ship, a brown-coloured bird-of-prey soared. Perhaps a hawk or kite, it glided in a circle before briefly flapping its wings to propel further ahead. We had indeed seen many interesting creatures in Papua New Guinea, many of which had close genetic links with corresponding species found in Australia. This was not surprising given that it was believed to be the home of many undocumented species of plants and animals. Later on in the night I would see a huge moth, black with a white stripe on each wing, and the size of my hand.

As the early morning turned to late, I was once again paired with Brett on motorboat duty. Now it was my turn to take the helm of one of the Falcon RHIBs. It was my time to learn and become experienced in such a field. I was tasked with following a line across a GPS device. This navigation system also pointed out where the water was shallow and deep, and I would take care not to go near the red zones. Those indicated either a coral reef or a sunken ship. Such wrecks could have ranged from an accident in modern times to a casualty of World War II. I do not remember the name of the village that we had arrived at. All I know is that we were docked on a small cliff just short of it. I was tasked with watching over the boat as Brett went into the village. At one point, somebody's wooden boat came alarmingly close to the Falcon's port side. I waded into the water hastily and stopped it before its long, sharp bow could pierce the rubber. I dreaded to think what would happen if I didn't intercept it in time, for I would have been given the evil eye the rest of the trip. A long time later, Brett returned with some passengers that would be taken to the medical ship, and I took the helm again. I was beginning to feel the pressure of navigating this boat and making sure it wasn't damaged, thanks in no small part to one of the Falcon boats being damaged prior and unable to move before today had even began. Therefore, I did feel quite a shock when I ventured too close to one of the red zones. So close that you could see the coral under the sea reaching out like claws and inciting an exclamation of alarm from some of the passengers. Brett told me not to be sorry and instead learn from the mistake.

My lunch was a sandwich that I had left in the storage compartment wrapped in plastic, making it hot in the wrong way. Then, in the afternoon we would make our way back with several others, and with Brett carrying an old guitar of his that he was going to gift to a local boy who had a greater passion for music than him. When I disembarked into waist high water, I forgot my phone was still in my pocket. The saltwater would ruin my rear camera and deny further selfies on this trip. I did need to update to one of the more modern phones anyway.

On the outreach, each day presented its share of fascinating sights, yet the promise of tomorrow held the prospect of an even more extraordinary experience. Venturing outside the door to the decks, I was poised to witness a sight that would leave me breathless. It was as if I were stepping into the pages of *Robinson Crusoe* or *The Lost World*. The emerald green hills that stretched before me held an air of mystery and enchantment, and the revelation of the lettering on one hillside unveiled the destination, Tufi, situated on the southeastern peninsula of Cape Nelson in Oro Province.

Tufi was nestled on one of the many rias, or drowned river valleys locally known as 'fjords,' and graced the cape with its presence. Captain Jan, being from a land full of fjords, used that nickname which stuck with the rest of us. Above, one could see the Tufi Dive Resort. The surrounding landscape, dotted with uncharted reefs, added an element of intrigue and challenge to our maritime exploration. As the ship set course for Tufi, anticipation and awe filled the conversations of those nearby me, awaiting an unparalleled encounter with the natural wonders of this remote and enchanting corner of the world.

The boat came up to a floating dock with a wooden platform extending into clear, tropical waters. The structure near the water was a simple roofed design, possibly a boathouse or storage facility for marine equipment or supplies. The YWAM uniform-clad volunteers carried containers off, likely engaged in logistical or transport activities. Locals could be seen along a pathway near the waterline, indicative of light community or work-related activities.

The views continued to be spectacular. The mighty ria cliffs, carved by volcanic activity, dwarfed the medical ship standing beside them. I wondered how many of the ship's donors and sponsors fully realised this grand sight. The volunteers would step onto the wooden raft platforms carrying their boxes or supplies, while local children swam within netted boundaries.

Later on, we went at awesome speed along clear water around and deep into the fjords where we would see even greater tapestries of rainforest fauna. The boat pulled up into a quiet, verdant inlet in a dense mangrove forest where trees grew directly out of the still, brackish water. The exposed roots of one large mangrove tree were particularly striking, a reminder of how these plants cling to both land and water, forming the biological backbone of the coastline.

In water calm and clear, reflecting the green foliage, our blue inflatable boat pulled up to some traditional dugout canoes tied to the bank, like a blend of modern utility and traditional life common across the Oro Province.

Palm trees and low jungle brush rose on the slopes beyond, hinting at the steep terrain typical of Tufi's geography. The greenery is thick and uninterrupted. Sure enough, nearby was a path leading to civilisation amidst the seemingly infinite forest. I would hike with others while Brett guarded the boat. The hike would become a pretty arduous one over time. The path was long, and the heat was stifling. The threat of jungle infections was never far off. The view beyond, however, was a great reward, showcasing the many hills and branching river paths. One that many others wouldn't see. I got close enough to see some kind of homestead, with garden rows in the foreground, probably kaukau, taro, or yam, which are staple crops in Oro Province, along with decorative shrubs and flowering coconut palms and a thatched house just visible beyond the trees.

Around there, I reached the point where I would have to leave the team to carry on into the distance and go back down. They disappeared up the path with their supply boxes, and I was left with admiration for them, going the distance. I was alone in the uninhabited rainforest. The isolation and solitude were heavy. For the most part, I was on a high vantage point overlooking calm, deep-blue water cradled between lush, steep hills draped in tropical vegetation. The hills were blanketed in thick jungle and kunai grass, typical of the high-rainfall zones of the Cape Nelson Peninsula.

The immediate trees suggested I was near a cultivated zone or a footpath between hamlets. Aside from that, there was no sign of modern infrastructure, just untouched landscape. The isolation was part of what makes this region such a powerful experience for visitors and a lifeline for locals when medical teams arrive.

Back on the ship, I spent my break time resting with some others in the lounge room. I was sharing the couches with a group of women who had clearly formed their own circle before or during the trip. As the conversation led up to it, I showcased some peaceful music I enjoyed listening to. *Call of the Ancients* by a Finnish independent composer was a majestic symphony of Celtic flute and harp music. The two instruments blended to form a brilliant, gentle melody, prompting the same woman I toured Oro Bay with to encourage the others into a small meditation. It was a similar practise that I would do over the years as the stress and anxiety would close in on me in various moments, from study to writing. It's moments like those that remind me to come back to myself amidst the wide world, even as my neurodivergent mind had trouble slowing down or overthinking. That evening, I found a new favourite soft drink in the form of 7Up. The text on the can it came in was in Tok Pisin, which was as interesting as it was amusing!

The view outside was also nothing short of amazing as beyond the windows was a sight of fjords and palm trees and green hills. To this day, I'm still amazed I was there to see such a sight. One would probably expect it from an extravagant ocean liner, not really a medical ship. Even so, the ship turning around with the flow of the water did make a few people slightly dizzy and seasickness was indeed flowing among some of the people unfamiliar with sea travel.

A sailor's son like me was unfazed, which was just as well because the seas tomorrow would be much rougher than they were in the morning. An unpleasant surprise for me in my turn to be at the helm for I struggled to keep the ship on course and navigate the rough waves. Brett was at his toughest yet, giving me instructions, repeating his usual line of "don't muck about!" Only this time, he wasn't saying "muck." I was pretty shaken up by the time we were at the lagoon again, realising being the rookie of the team could get pretty rough at times. Life is filled with times like that. Times that will indeed be rough enough to test you, make you wonder why you did this, but if a volunteer wants to make a difference, they must not be afraid. They must be their best in the roughest waters. I kicked in that mindset on the way back as the missionary team got back in and put their safety into my hands as I grasped the helm. Then, when I finally asked Brett if he'd take over, he did. It turned out I could have asked at any time, as I was still learning. Indeed, I was learning in more ways than one what it meant to be a volunteer.

That night, the ship was moving again. This time, I saw the displays of the ship's bridge as the autopilot navigated its way through the dark. Each screen displayed our position in various ways, while a paper map of the peninsula of Tufi was bathed in lamp light.

By first light tomorrow, the second phase of the outreach would begin in earnest.

Chapter Four

Papua New Guinea Part II – The Village and the Port

The morning would reveal the ship was moving again. I would see a sponsor's list on the wall of the ship's midsection. There were the flags showing the Gulf, Western, Central, Oro, Milne Bay and Morobe provincial governments. There were also those of the Australian companies ranging from dentists, media, property groups, charities, alongside the PNG Ports Corporation, Port of Townsville, the North Queensland Cowboys, and more. There was the City of Townsville logo, an abstract icon of sailing boats on a blue sea with a brown Castle Hill in the background – a home that felt so far away now. Looking outside to the seashore and nameless hills beyond showed just how far these generous donations had reached. While helping a ship go to such places may have seemed simple from a map's view of the course, the reality was a grand one beyond imagination. It was the power of volunteering and charity that propelled this ship across a far corner of the world.

These small icons were the only remnant of home aboard the ship. We were no longer in the blissful, homely community of Townsville City, but instead cruising the waves to an unknown place. There were more worlds than one, many of us on board truly realised now. The Solomon Sea, the Owen Stanley Range, the shores of the Papuan Peninsula. Those are another world, one completely distinct from ours…

Speaking of which, the next place would be the most unexplored yet, according to what I was told at the time. The boat slowed from its cruise and made its way toward the part of the shore containing the small village of Manau, in the Tamata Rural LLG at the northern edge of Oro Province. Nestled in a seemingly nameless bay flanked by the Mambare River to the south and the Gira River to the north, very, very little is known of this settlement. Many small villages in Papua New Guinea are quite isolated and not widely documented anyhow, especially with over 800 languages and many small communities. Looking it up online yields next to no results for those in the outside world, not even with the help of modern AI. Think about it… If you're connected to volunteer or research projects in the area, you may have access to knowledge that hasn't yet been shared widely online.

While there was a motorboat of villagers that came in to greet us, and perhaps the occasional fishing canoe, the forest straddling the shore was still and silent. There was no wharf, no roads, no facilities on the beach, and no planes in the sky. This was truly an uncharted place in the world, in every sense of the word, and I was among the select few who would ever visit this part of the planet…

A TIME FOR VOLUNTEERS

The next morning, which was a Sunday, would see me and many others go on to the beach, and walk a path cut through the tall grass and palm trees to Manau proper. More traditional houses would greet us as we entered the village. Villages in Papua New Guinea often feature traditional stilted houses made from local materials like palm wood and thatch. These communities are sometimes involved in volunteer-based efforts, with a focus on sustainability, education, and healthcare. If you're working or volunteering in a village like Manau, you're likely contributing to vital development efforts in one of the most remote and richly biodiverse regions of the world.

The locals greeted us enthusiastically, and we gathered in the local church. This church comprised of a wooden altar, beautiful flower decorations, a roof of palm fronds damaged in part from a recent storm, and wooden seats. We sat down and attended the morning mass which was sung with great enthusiasm from the locals. It was an uplifting sight, seeing all their happy expressions and eager singing as they carried on. There were sermons too, and together, they seemingly went on for a while. It honestly felt a little bit longer after sitting on that wooden plank, but that meant little. This was a unique experience I would never forget.

From there, I explored the rest of the town. Dad would take some pictures of chickens, a dog, a small pig, and of himself with some locals. Flowers and fruit were being grown. There were some modern structures as well as the traditional housing and a water pump, implying that there had been a prominent building effort from visitors to create something for this town. That said, the other houses were nothing short of impressive themselves. Again, they were elevated on stilts crafted from the various wood of the trees beyond. The floor was smoothly paved sand and very tidy. Some houses were walled in, while others were open in the form of some kind of gathering place. Palm trees formed a clear boundary, gently swaying in the summer breeze. There was even a two-story building made entirely through the same techniques as the rest of the houses. My dad and I were amazed at the handiwork of the villagers; It spoke a lot about what they were capable of, and how much they cared for their collective community to create such amazing houses. This was the power of community in plain sight. It didn't matter what tools or resources you had. Many hands make a house, and many more hands make a bigger house. This village, while distant, was very much alive.

That night we were on another form of gangway watch. This time, our station was at the bridge. During our shifts, each of us would sit and watch the various systems, followed by a patrol of the ship every hour in the manner of a security job. I will never forget the sheer stillness of those nights. The ship's floodlights illuminated the immediate surroundings. That was a rare gift for the fishermen in their canoes who could now see the green water penetrated by light. Aside from that, that was the only artificial lighting in the entire area, as beyond the deck was a complete darkness, illuminated only by the moon.

My only companion was my phone as it began the long journey that was the audiobook of Ernest Hemingway's, *Islands in the Stream*. Published posthumously, I found it to be an inspiration not just in the Thomas Hudson character's life in all three acts, but also how it was found and brought to light long after its author passed. Out there, in the wilderness, I could enjoy it without any distractions, immediate or far away.

My father told me something he felt while he was on his shift. As he took a walk around, he saw the moonlit view beyond. Then, for the first time in a long time, he thought of... nothing. Nothing about the future and nothing about the past. Nothing immediate and nothing beyond. Hearing him talk about it made me realise that I thought about nothing too, and how there is never enough time in the world to do all the nothing you want. Here in Manau we had a great experience of nothing, yet to the locals, it was their everything.

The next two days were the usual ship duties. There weren't many remarkable moments to share. Some missionaries and doctors went ashore, but we were not among them. At one point on the second day, Dad, Toby, and I were on the ship's foredeck and saw YWAM's own EC145 helicopter in the distance. It descended to a landing point then took off presumably to Popondetta. As an aviation student, I would have loved to be with those flying missionaries, flying in treacherous skies across a labyrinth of high mountains and low valleys where only the native birds dare to fly.

Later in the day, there was another sunset through towering cumulonimbus clouds. This sunset was like no other, as only a few will ever see it in this form. It was a rare and tremendous honour to contribute to Manau. Even in the far reaches of Earth, humanity finds a way to live, and that is worth volunteering for.

The YWAM Medical Ship, that was our home during this trip, is 60 metres long and carries over 120 people, yet she still felt like a Nimitz-class aircraft carrier compared to any boats in the Sailing Club. She operates in remote areas and therefore needed to be fully independent, especially in the area of fire safety. In order to ensure the crew are prepared for any fire dangers, they must practice drills and maintain firefighting equipment. These duties fell to the specialist boat crew who were also responsible for the operation and maintenance of all deck equipment, the main engines, the inflatable boat support vessels, and the steerage and navigation of the ship. While many of these crew have commercial shipping experience, they still needed to practice operating as a team and to train those volunteers who were new to these duties.

The ship has some automatic fire fighting systems including sprinklers. However, the specialist crew may need to enter parts of the ship with fire hoses and extinguishers and perhaps rescue fellow crew members who may have been overcome by smoke or who may be injured and unable to evacuate the fire area. So, the crew train and practice working in small groups. When alerted of a fire, they rush to areas where the firefighting equipment is stored. One crew member will assist another to get dressed into fireproof heat-resistant trousers and overcoats and then a hard hat, a face shield and self-contained breathing equipment. While this is happening, another pair will remove a fire hose from its storage and unroll it on the deck to ensure it has no blockages. It is then connected to the high-pressure water pump system. Having dressed the leader, the second person then also dresses in the protective clothing. The leader grabs the hose and with his offsider close behind, they enter the space where the fire is located to fight the fire. Other crew may collect portable fire extinguishers and fight any smaller flames.

Away from the fire, a senior officer will be communicating with all the fire fighters by radio and using their feedback to co-ordinate the best tactic to fight the fire. This can include closing off fireproof doors in various compartments so the fire is starved of oxygen and dies off.

An important drill is rescuing any injured or disorientated crew. The engine rooms and bilge areas are in the very lowest parts of the ship. The crew there may need to be rescued, or the fire may be in those compartments. To do this the leader and offsider must descend the stairs into those areas and other crew will support by ensuring the hose does not get caught and can be easily pulled forward by the lead pair. Having fought the fire and located the injured crew they must then

A TIME FOR VOLUNTEERS

assess the injuries and determine the best way to transport the crew member to the main deck and onto the medical rooms for treatment. The balance of the crew including the captain would then enter the affected area and determine what repairs are needed.

When all is over, the equipment must be folded up, the hoses rolled up, and all stored very carefully in a particular way to ensure they can be efficiently accessed next time they are needed.

The daily ship routine included a Programme Maintenance diary which lists all types of equipment all over the ship which must be checked and maintained on a regular basis. Some items were inspected every few days while others need less frequent inspection. This includes the firefighting equipment.

For those volunteers who had not experienced this type of firefighting training and equipment before, this training is a valuable education and one that may prove useful in later life. Learning new skills and the use of equipment one has not experienced before are some of the many benefits volunteers receive from giving of their time to worthy causes. Who knows when such knowledge may prove useful to your future employment or social enjoyment? The friendships and sense of team building also gives volunteers a sense of belonging that contributes to one's life purpose and satisfaction.

In the after hours, I found solace in scrolling through social media on one of the shared computers again. The news from home brought a mix of welcome updates and reminders that stirred unwanted emotions. It was during this interlude that a poignant lesson emerged, one of focusing on what I could control and letting go of the anxieties associated with the external world. Even then, I wondered why I was concerning myself with that, realising the futility of worrying about elements beyond my influence. This realisation prompted a significant shift in my online habits, leading me to personally abstain from perusing my Facebook feed, recognising the detrimental impact of negativity on my mental well-being. The decision proved transformative, with the absence of this digital noise contributing to a noticeable reduction in anxiety and an overall improvement in my life.

Nevertheless, a post emerged on that day, offering a timely dose of motivation. Shared by my close friend and (though she didn't know it at the time) fellow author, Rebeccah Statham, the post featured her looking out to a background between two large rocks toward an enigmatic shore. The accompanying text resonated with a philosophical intent, advocating a profound acceptance of one's authentic self.

"I want to know that at the end of the day I was no one else but me.

I don't want to spend my hours, days, or my life trying to be something other than who I am.

We underestimate the person we are deep down. The real you. The one that makes stupid jokes. The you that wants to dance in the middle of the street, the real you that has all these huge dreams bursting to explode into real life, the real you that wants to do something other than what you're doing currently.

Our job isn't to be superheroes. To have huge houses & big careers. Our job is to live every day as (insert your name here). I want to be as me as I can every single day. And you should want to be you too. Because you're special, and only you can be you."

This served as a reminder to embrace the quirks, dreams, and aspirations that define the core of our being, the unfiltered essence that makes us uniquely ourselves. Rebeccah's words, a beacon of wisdom amidst the digital tumult, reinforced the empowering notion that our primary task in life is not to conform to external expectations but to live authentically, for we are each special in our own right.

Rebeccah is now a thriving author and business consultant. While she has embarked on a successful journey, the moments and simple acts of kindness from that pivotal point in time continue to resonate for many. The gratitude for these gestures lingers, a silent acknowledgment of the profound influence that supportive friendships can wield. In the unique context of Papua New Guinea, even in a place unknown to the entire internet, the ripple effect of such acts of kindness becomes even more apparent. It serves as a poignant reminder that connections forged, even in the most remote corners of the world, can transcend time and space. The echoes of mateship and encouragement, whether in the digital realms or the landscapes of Papua New Guinea, underscore the far-reaching impact of genuine human connection.

That night, I was on deck watch again at midnight. The displays showed our position, such as the one showing us drifting around at 0.10 knots with our stern at 261 degrees true and bow at 176 degrees true. The only noises were the humming of the engines and small chatter down the hall. Another screen showed the various Gensets of the power to the engines, with the first trackball I'd ever seen, and security feed to the screen to the right. The helm was a small steering wheel with a compass and digital display. Radio equipment was to the right. The most eerie display was the depth sonar. Out here, the sea floor was a complete enigma. I remember looking at any orange patch that would scroll from one side to the other, mystified.

Then, a small alarm went off. Looking at the SAILOR 6103 Alarm Panel, red text reading *"MF/HR 1 ▫ Distress"* appeared, with the *"Distress"* flashing. In the range of radio frequencies from 300 kHz to 3 MHz, which is often used for marine communication, there was an emergency situation, most likely elsewhere in the Solomon Sea.

Captain Jan came in, still in his uniform, and took note of the details of the distress signal. Then, he returned to his office. I would later hear that it was some kind of Singaporean ship that had run into nearby trouble. Unfortunately, we were in no position to assist, and even if we were, we weren't a rescue vessel designed for such a task.

The oceans, particularly around Papua, can be perilous. Covering two-thirds of our planet, their vastness is matched by our limited understanding. Yet the ocean is far from being a barren expanse; it is a bustling realm where 50 million people work at any given time. Much of this activity is fraught with risk and, at times, illegality. The ocean has long been perceived as a frontier beyond the reach of terrestrial laws and governments, a place where anything can happen. Sea slavery, gunrunning, overfishing, illegal fishing, dumping, and piracy are all too common. The rest of the seafarers, such as us, have to be aware of it, lest we run into our own emergencies.

Papua New Guinea is no exception. The maritime element of its defence force is severely underfunded, making the task of patrolling such a vast Exclusive Economic Zone daunting. They heavily rely on daily reports from US satellite surveillance to monitor the presence of foreign ships. Our hope is that Australia will continue to assist in patrolling these waters and in training navy personnel.

Volunteers, like these crews, venture into these ungoverned and perhaps ungovernable waters, exploring the planet's last frontier. In places like these, we're on our own for the most part.

The next day was more of the usual. Highlights included seeing a moth so thick and huge on the raindrop-covered railing that it bore a resemblance to Mothra, and reading *Part Two: Masters of War* of *Winter Hawk*. Its opening quote was from Bob Dylan's, *Shelter from the Storm*, appropriate for most of our shipborne duties and volunteering to help people shelter indeed.

On the 3rd of February, under pouring rain and cloudy mist, covering us from the rest of the world, I had a look in our medical bay where nurses and doctors worked meticulously on helping locals with all manner of health problems. For them, it was a deliverance.

That night, more fishermen were indulging in the ship's lights illuminating her broadside. I saw wooden canoes with single-side floats with a rower on each end and various people sitting on a log bed in the middle. For my walkaround, the only thing I could see in the dark yonder was the moon, either close to or at full phase, and its shimmer on the water like a staircase to the horizon of a world that no longer seemed small. Again, for the first time in a long time, I thought nothing. In this busy world, where we are working, active, or online at any given time, moments like these are as increasingly uncommon as they are welcoming. I would walk to the bow, equally inert, and the stern area where fuel drums and the motorboats sat motionless in their storage. It was perfect stillness, and even that had its wonders.

On the 4th, Lae was coming into view. Sitting near the delta of the Markham River and at the start of the Highlands Highway, the capital of Morobe Province and second largest city in the country was a gateway to the Highlands Region and the coast. As such, it is the largest cargo port of the country and the industrial hub of Papua New Guinea. It was especially grand by the scale of the rest of the Morobe Province.

The buildings and antenna towers among the trees were a large city area in comparison to the other places we visited. Further ahead, thick clouds covered the mountain range, and a massive wall of rain was to the south. The ship made its way across the water full of scattered container ships, bringing supplies to and from the main city of the northern part of the nation. The yellow pilot boat guided us in. Shipping companies such as Kyowa Line could be seen on the sides of the container ships as we cruised slowly in. Finally, the ship came to berth next to an area of flat ground with some stacked containers, and behind us was the MV *Bougainville Coast*, the same ship we saw in Alotau, sitting moored like a resting titan.

Then, it was time for one last sleep. The *Bougainville Coast* cruised past on its own journey. I walked around the illuminated deck, still and silent, one last time. Even the port of Lae had its quiet moments.

At dawn, we all said our goodbyes and Dad and I hopped into one of two Toyota HiAce vans that would take us to the Lae Nadzab Airport which was forty-two kilometres away. It was a sunny and humid morning in the Garden City, as it is usually year-round. The city boasts several notable landmarks and institutions. The lush greenery and abundant rainfall contribute to the city's vibrant natural surroundings. However, the heavy rains can also lead to infrastructure challenges such as flooding and road maintenance issues.

Despite these challenges, Lae remains a dynamic city with a growing population and economy. The city's markets, such as the popular Lae Market, offer a wide variety of fresh produce, crafts, and goods, reflecting the rich cultural diversity of the region. Additionally, Lae hosts several annual events and festivals that celebrate the local culture and heritage. The University of Technology is one of Papua New Guinea's premier educational institutions, offering a range of technical and engineering programs. The Lae War Cemetery is a sombre reminder of the city's role in World War II, commemorating the soldiers who fought and died in the region. The nearby Mount Lunaman offers scenic views of the city and surrounding areas.

We soon reached the Highlands Highway, also known as Okuk Highway, a vital land route that connects several major cities and facilitates the movement of people and goods between the densely populated Highlands region and the coast. This highway is the lifeline of the area, enabling the transport of essential supplies and agricultural products, and serving as a key artery for commerce and daily life.

However, for most of its length, the Highlands Highway is merely a single carriageway two-lane road, often plagued by potholes and landslips. These road conditions can make travel slow and hazardous, and the journey is further complicated by the frequent occurrence of armed hold-ups and robberies committed by local raskol bandits, particularly in the more remote and isolated sections of the Highlands region.

Fortunately, we encountered no raskols during our journey, likely because we were traveling during the day when the risk is generally lower. However, the poor condition of the highway presented its own challenges. The van had to slow to a crawl in several places as we navigated through large potholes and sections of road that had been completely gouged out, forcing the driver to weave through the least damaged parts of the dirt track. The rough, muddy river bridges and dense rainforest gradually gave way to the rolling hinterland, a landscape marked by steep hills and lush vegetation. Despite the road's difficulties, the journey offered glimpses of the region's rugged natural beauty, with views of distant mountains and verdant valleys.

Finally, we reached Nadzab Airport which has served both private and regional aircraft with domestic flights since replacing Lae Airfield in 1977. Located on the Erap River, 5 kilometres north of the Markham River, the airport is neighboured by the settlements of Gabmatsung and Gabsonkek to the east.

Nadzab Airport is not only significant today, but also historically important. On September 5th, 1943, it was the site of a historic airborne landing by the US Army's 503rd Parachute Infantry Regiment and elements of the Australian Army's 2/4th Field Regiment in the Markham Valley, observed by General Douglas MacArthur himself, circling overhead in a B-17. This operation, in conjunction with the amphibious landing east of Malahang, marked the beginning of the liberation of Lae from Japanese occupation. That same day, the Australian 2/2nd Pioneer Battalion, 2/6th Field Company, and Papuan Infantry Battalion reached Nadzab after an overland and river trek and began preparing the airfield.

Despite wet weather challenges, the road to Nadzab was opened on December 15, 1943. Nadzab then became a major Allied air base in New Guinea, hosting numerous United States Army Air Forces and Royal Australian Air Force units. It served as a forward base of operations against Japanese positions and later as a staging area. Two parallel runways were constructed, running east to west: Number 1 Strip to the north, and Number 2 Strip closer to the Markham River, to the south. In 1962, the Australian Commonwealth Department of Works resealed and lengthened the main strip at Nadzab to accommodate Mirage fighters had the occasion arisen. The Australian Department of Civil Aviation maintained it as an alternative to Lae in poor weather conditions.

Today, the former East Base or No. 1 and No. 2 runways are still in civilian use, mainly servicing Lae, which is 45 kilometres away. Roads in the area built by American forces remain in place. Nadzab Airport was redeveloped by Australia in the early to mid-1970s as an independence gift to Papua New Guinea in 1975 and became operational in 1977.

While writing this, I learned that it is now officially Nadzab Tomodachi International Airport. As the Post-Courier reported on 20 April 2023, it was renamed to symbolise the cooperation and friendship between the people of Japan and Papua New Guinea. The word "Tomodachi" means "friend" in Japanese. The renaming was announced by the Minister of Transport and Civil Aviation during the unveiling of a plaque by the Japanese International Cooperation Agency.

The historical significance of Nadzab for both nations was not overlooked during the renaming ceremony. As officials witnessed the transformation of Nadzab into a modern international airport, they were reminded of the long period of peace and prosperity the world has enjoyed and the enduring friendship and economic cooperation between Japan and Papua New Guinea.

I am quite impressed and pleased with this development. Anyone capable of achieving such a feat in Papua is truly extending their reach in the world. The redevelopment of Nadzab is not only symbolically significant but also enhances social and economic development in the region, and the nation as a whole. With the nation so difficult to traverse that its main cities aren't connected by road, aviation plays a crucial role in the social and economic development, as seen in the three volumes of James Sinclair's *Balus: The Aeroplane of Papua New Guinea*. Now, they are looking to see if Tokua Airport in East New Britain Province can be developed similarly to boost tourism in the region. I would like to see that.

Finally, our ride to Port Moresby arrived, a Bombardier Dash 8 operated by PNG Air. The tail featured a colourful and abstract design with various geometric shapes and stylized faces in a palette of black, white, red, and yellow. The artwork is reminiscent of traditional and contemporary motifs, blending cultural elements into a modern aesthetic. As we boarded the plane, the intricate designs reflected the rich cultural heritage of Papua New Guinea, adding a unique touch to our journey. Up ahead, the sky was partly cloudy with a mix of white and grey clouds, allowing glimpses of blue sky. Below, the landscape was lush and green, typical of the region's tropical climate. On the distant horizon was mountainous terrain shrouded in low-lying clouds, adding depth to the scene. The flight took us over the Highlands towards Port Moresby, offering breathtaking views as the plane climbed higher. Looking down, we could see the mighty Markham River snaking through the landscape like a great titan, a reminder of the rugged and untamed beauty of the region.

During the flight, I leafed through the PNG Air Magazine which provided an intriguing glimpse into the vibrant culture and events of Papua New Guinea. The magazine featured articles on the 60th Kokoda Crossing, a significant commemoration of the historic World War II trail, as well as Papua New Guinea's first War Canoe Festival, a celebration of traditional maritime heritage. It also highlighted the burgeoning surfing scene in Papua New Guinea, showcasing the pristine waves that are attracting surfers before the rest of the world catches on. The content was a fascinating window into the diverse and rich world of life in Papua New Guinea, both past and present.

As we flew over the majestic Owen Stanley Range, the sight of the towering mountains was awe-inspiring. The rugged peaks and deep valleys, often shrouded in mist, are a testament to the challenging terrain that has shaped the history and culture of the region. The Owen Stanley Range is not just a natural wonder but also a symbol of resilience and endurance, having played a significant role during World War II. The view from the plane, with the sun casting shadows over the jagged ridges, was a fitting end to our journey through the Highlands and a reminder of the incredible landscapes that Papua New Guinea has to offer.

We had finally come full circle, arriving back at Port Moresby International Airport. I distinctly remember the unsettling sight of various firearm silhouettes at the Clearance Lodgement and Pickup Point which said a thing or two of the security concerns in the region. The duty-free section was quite impressive to me. There was a noticeable emphasis on pearls, with displays showcasing majestic silver varieties that were truly captivating.

A TIME FOR VOLUNTEERS   91

On the Air Niugini flight to Cairns, I took another look at the in-flight magazine. It featured advertisements for Heli Niugini, highlighting the essential role helicopters play in such a mountainous country. There were also ads for Heineken, Honiara's finest hotel, and Oro Province, reminding me of the places we had just visited. In the "Events" section, I noticed the Supercar races in Townsville, known back then as the Castrol Edge Townsville 400. It was heartening to see how far the efforts of fellow volunteers who participated in that event were recognized, reaching audiences far and wide. There was also a photo of the PNG Kumuls rugby team and a group of volunteers from NCS showing a banner *"We believe violence against women hurts the whole family,"* demonstrating the strong community spirit of volunteers in Papua New Guinea.

For those who love adventure in Oceania, Port Moresby serves as a gateway to fascinating destinations like Chuuk, Pohnpei, Honiara, Port Vila, and Nadi. The airport connects these places to larger cities such as Cairns, Brisbane, Sydney, Singapore, Denpasar, Manila, Kuala Lumpur, Auckland, and even as far as Hong Kong, Shanghai, and Tokyo. The magazine also included Tok Pisin translations in the Visitor's Guide, profiles of Air Niugini's fleet, and much more, offering a comprehensive look at the travel opportunities from this key hub.

Finally, we landed in Cairns where we said goodbye to our fellow Townsville citizen, Doctor Lisa, before heading back home. It was the end of an enlightening journey filled with unforgettable experiences and new perspectives.

Over time, I've heard more stories about those volunteers working out in Papua New Guinea. My father returned to the ship in 2018, around the Central Province, continuing his usual deck crew duties.

More recently, the outreaches have commonly gone to the Western Province. Situated in the southwestern part of Papua New Guinea, it borders Indonesia's Highland Papua and South Papua Provinces to the west and lies adjacent to Australia's Cape York Peninsula across the Torres Strait. At approximately 98,000 square kilometres, it is the country's largest province, occupying roughly 21% of Papua New Guinea's total landmass.

But for all its size, the Western Province is one of the most isolated and impoverished regions in the country. Infrastructure is limited, and much of the province remains disconnected by roads or regular services. The outreach efforts focus primarily along the Fly River—an enormous, winding artery that cuts through thick jungle and vast swamp. The river and its tributaries serve as lifelines to dozens of remote villages, but navigating it is no easy task. The environment is harsh, humid, and often unpredictable. It's a place where travel is slow, communication is difficult, and support is scarce.

Despite these conditions, volunteers and missionaries persist in their efforts to bring medical care, education, and community support to the people living there. These teams work tirelessly—often with little recognition—to reach those on the fringes of modern services. What might seem like small victories from afar—treating a wound, delivering supplies, providing a safe birth—can be life-changing moments in such remote areas.

In many ways, the work being done here is a quiet kind of heroism. The kind that doesn't make headlines but leaves a lasting impact in the lives it touches. Maybe someday I'll join them there.

It was during 2017 that I discovered my talent and love for volunteer work, especially in the tropics. The thrill of adventure and joy in contributing to a better world are the best parts for me. Every day was one of challenges, duties, and endurance. That is what makes them so epic in hindsight. The jungles and seas proved to be worthy opponents. You had to earn your right to be there, through the weather, terrain, and ever-present threat of natural infections. People who have ventured there have many stories to tell, and I was no exception.

The seemingly distant narrative of our maritime adventures in Papua New Guinea, particularly the lessons learned, and experiences gained in the remote reaches of Tufi, might appear disconnected from the context of floods. Yet, as the story unfolds, the threads of connection will become apparent. The intricacies of volunteering in Papua New Guinea, navigating uncharted territories, and adapting to diverse environments would play a pivotal role in shaping the readiness and resilience required for the challenges that lay ahead.

Fast forward to February 2019, and the echoes of those lessons learned in Papua New Guinea would resound with a newfound significance. The skills developed in the remote landscapes of Tufi, where uncharted reefs posed challenges, and the ability to adapt to diverse and unfamiliar surroundings would prove invaluable. The journey from Papua New Guinea to the flood-stricken landscapes of 2019 illustrates the interconnectedness of experiences and the transferability of skills cultivated through volunteering. As the narrative unfolds, the bridge between these seemingly disparate events will become clear, revealing the universal themes of preparedness, adaptability, and resilience.

Chapter Five

The Distant Thunder of Paluma

Two years would pass after Papua New Guinea, and what an eventful two years they were. In July, I would go on to study at the International Summer Program at Korea Aerospace University in Goyang. There, my unique stories would fascinate many a fellow student as we explored the bustling night life of Seoul, the demilitarized zone, and many other tourist spots around the Republic of Korea. Then, I'd finish my Diploma of Aviation with high distinctions and eventually receive it in Bundaberg in 2018.

Come 2019, and the lessons and memories of Papua New Guinea, always fresh in my mind, would return.

The onslaught of heavy rains that eventually led to the devastating floods caught many residents off guard, seemingly appearing out of nowhere and affecting every corner of the city. While the Bureau of Meteorology had issued flash flood warnings, as they usually did with paramount authority, the extent of the flooding still came as a shocking blow to the people residing in the suburbs at the time.

Remarkably, I had noticed some subtle warning signs, albeit not the most prominent ones. There were fleeting glimpses of what lay ahead, indicating that something extraordinary was brewing. My personal encounter with this massive and unconventional monsoon had already commenced in the misty mountains of the Paluma Range National Park.

During the Australia Day weekend, a customary tradition for my father and me involved embarking on a camping trip to Lake Paluma. As members of the Townsville Sailing Club, we joined several other enthusiasts who converged on the lake for this annual event. Our days were filled with exhilarating sails, while the evenings were spent gathered around crackling campfires, engaged in animated conversations.

The Village in the Clouds was brought to life by a modest community of around thirty permanent residents who welcomed a steady stream of visitors, drawn by the allure of the southernmost point of Townsville's Wet Tropics. Rooted in history, the old town's origins can be traced back to the tales of mining and forestry, their lineage leading to the prospectors of the 1870s, driven by the pursuit of tin riches hidden within the mountains. The evolution of the area remained a quiet narrative until a road, gradually etched into the terrain, emerged in the 1930s, finally connecting this hidden haven with the outside world.

In earlier times, the range stood as a demarcation between distinct Aboriginal linguistic groups, often marking the boundary between the Gugu Badhun to the east and the Nawagi to the north. In the traditional Nawagi parlance, the Paluma Range was known as Munan Gumburu, aptly translating to "misty mountain." The nomenclature proved fitting as the shroud of morning mists often cloaked its peaks, enhancing its enigmatic beauty.

Far below the range, the historic Mount Spec Road and its stone-faced arched bridge spanning Little Crystal Creek bore testament to their longevity since 1933. This arch road bridge, an architectural relic, retained its functional importance as the sole operational bridge of its kind in the state. The Little Crystal Creek, perpetually replenished by crystal-clear waters that cascaded down from the heights, bestowed upon it a series of deep pools that had naturally shaped into an idyllic swimming hole. This aquatic gem held a special place in the hearts of many throughout North Queensland, offering respite and connection with nature's embrace. Many people from, and sometimes beyond, the surrounding local regions would visit the area in search for a getaway from the mundane busyness of normal life.

The Paluma Dam was part of a unique water supply system that used gravity to feed megalitres of water per day to the city of Townsville. For most of the year, water flowing from the Mount Spec part of the national park was collected and filtered at the Crystal Creek intake and then piped under gravity to Townsville. When Crystal Creek water levels were low, water was released into the creek from Lake Paluma via another gravity pipeline.

Lake Paluma was nestled among World Heritage-listed wet tropics rainforest. The pristine lake served as a sanctuary for a range of nature-based recreational activities such as canoeing, sailing, and swimming, offering visitors a serene escape from the hustle and bustle of everyday life. The journey to Lake Paluma was part of the adventure, with the lake only accessible via a twelve-kilometre gravel road just past the quaint township of Paluma.

Once there, visitors found themselves welcomed by well-maintained facilities, including picnic shelters and barbecues, perfect for enjoying a day out in nature. The area was a haven for wildlife enthusiasts, with many creatures calling the vast, dense rainforest home. Among them were the elusive platypus, the swift peregrine falcon, and the striking eastern water dragon. The diverse range of rainforest fauna added to the allure of the lake, making it a prime location for birdwatching and wildlife spotting.

Surrounded by the rich biodiversity and lush greenery of the wet tropics rainforest, Lake Paluma was more than just a recreational spot; it was a reminder of the natural beauty and ecological importance of preserving such pristine environments. The tranquil waters and the dense canopy of trees provided a perfect backdrop for both relaxation and adventure, drawing nature lovers and outdoor enthusiasts alike to its serene shores.

Little did I know during that idyllic camping trip to Lake Paluma that the unfolding events would intertwine with the impending disaster of the floods, forever shaping my perception and personal connection to the region.

Paluma will always be a special place for me. It is my preferred getaway for temporary escape from civilisation. I have many memories of sailing to the far end of the lake and exploring the still, towering trees echoing with the many birds and cicadas. If the water level at the time permitted, I would also walk down on rocky slopes of the spillway and gaze down the long winding creek that carried on over the horizon and eventually to the Burdekin River. More recently, I have trekked to the awe-inspiring Crystal Creek falls, where the water slides down to a waterfall that takes it on its journey through the range. The clouds would usually cloak the massive gorges in a ghostly grey mist. This place really is an ageless portrait of the tropical world that North Queensland lies in.

The Mount Spec Drive is a winding road through a dense, misty forest, as seen from inside our Forester. The view was slightly obstructed by raindrops on the windshield as the rain came. The road ahead curved in all manner of turns, and was bordered by lush, verdant foliage typical of a tropical rainforest. The trees were tall and dense, with a variety of ferns, vines, and undergrowth visible through the mist. The atmosphere appeared humid and cool, characteristic of a rainforest environment. The road is narrow and appears to be well-maintained, with white and red reflective markers along the edges for safety. Such a scene captured the serene, yet somewhat eerie beauty of a rainforest during a misty rain, adding to the sense of adventure and natural splendour that accompanies a drive to Paluma.

The rain was quite heavy when we climbed, but that was nothing to worry about. Such downpours were common during the summer, and sometimes they even added to the enjoyment of the trip. When you're sailing, you're already likely to be wet from the water beneath you, so being drenched from above wasn't much of a bother.

However, as the day progressed and our car continued to climb into the range, the downpour intensified. I remember the car's wipers struggling at times to clear the deluge. Large drops of water, which had coalesced on the leaves of the trees, kept splattering against the windshield. As we ascended further, the fog and mist, for which Paluma is traditionally known, began to envelop us. Passing by Crystal Creek, we noticed people seemed to be enjoying the weather despite the rain. But as we continued through the village and reached the dirt road leading to the dam, I saw the road was gradually turning into mud. This was concerning, as it could mean the road might become too muddy to traverse, potentially cutting short our camping trip.

By the time we arrived at the campsite, the rain was pouring down with full force. It felt like a battle between the sky and the trees, as the rainforest canopy was continuously battered, resembling a shield under attack. The relentless downpour made it quite difficult to pitch our tent, with every attempt to secure it thwarted by the torrential rain and gusty winds. The ground quickly turned to mud, and the usually peaceful sounds of the forest were drowned out by the incessant drumming of raindrops on leaves and the rumble of thunder in the distance.

It was clear that this was no longer just typical summer rain; it had become something far more intense. The air was thick with humidity and the scent of wet earth and foliage. Our clothes clung to us, soaked through despite our best efforts to stay dry. The atmosphere was both exhilarating and daunting as we struggled against the elements to create a semblance of shelter.

Amidst the chaos, there was a certain beauty to the scene. The rain brought the forest to life in a different way with streams of water cascading down tree trunks and pooling into small, temporary rivulets. The leaves glistened, and the normally subdued colours of the rainforest were amplified, creating a vibrant, almost ethereal landscape.

Even so, the view of Lake Paluma could never be tarnished, but merely take on another form in that of a serene and misty scene. The lake was surrounded by lush greenery, with trees framing the view from the picnic area on both sides. The water was rippling from the constant rainfall. The sky was overcast, creating a tranquil and somewhat mysterious atmosphere, with low-hanging clouds and mist partially obscuring the distant shore and the forested area beyond the lake. The overall mood of the scene was peaceful and reflective, highlighting the natural beauty and calmness of Lake Paluma, were it not for the relentless rain.

Here, the world feels zoomed in, with every detail amplified by the enveloping rain. The dense rainforest seems to close in around us, each leaf and drop of water magnified in the immediate vicinity. The trees stand tall and resolute, their canopies forming a thick, protective layer above. The air is filled with the sound of rain striking leaves, the earthy scent of wet soil, and the occasional call of a hidden bird, creating an intimate connection with the natural world. Yet, as we look beyond, the rainforest appears endless, draping over mountains that stretch to the horizon. The mist and rain blur the boundaries between land and sky, giving the landscape a dreamlike quality. The rolling hills and valleys, cloaked in verdant foliage, seem to go on forever, a vast and unbroken expanse of greenery. Each peak and trough in the distance hints at unexplored depths and the boundless mystery of the wilderness. The juxtaposition of the immediate, detailed view and the infinite stretch of the rainforest creates a profound sense of awe. It's as if we are caught between two worlds: one where every raindrop and leaf is intimately known, and another where the majesty of nature extends beyond our comprehension. This duality heightens the experience, reminding us of the incredible scale and beauty of the environment around us.

I took a walk along the wall of the dam to the reservoir, wearing a thick raincoat my father usually reserved for sailing in thunderstorms. The clouds were everywhere, shrouding the rainforest in a dense layer of mist. The path along the dam was gravelly and wet from the rain, bordered by a metal guardrail on one side that was rough to the touch with rust. Large rocks lined the edge of the dam, providing stability and protection against the water even during its fury. The trees in the background were dense and lush, and the rain pattering against them was a massive chorus. Normally, this wouldn't have been an issue, but the rain, seemingly falling sideways, was relentless. It seemed like it could continue for days without letting up. The water in and around the dam was stirring, adding to the already eerie atmosphere created by the constant downpour and the enveloping mist. Despite the harsh conditions, there was a certain beauty to the scene. The mist clung to the trees, wrapping them in a ghostly embrace. The rain, while relentless, added a rhythmic beat to the atmosphere, a constant reminder of nature's power.

The view beyond was still incredible, even with reduced visibility, dominated by dense, lush forest, with layers of trees extending into the distance. The trees closest to the viewer were a mix of deep green and slightly lighter shades, indicating a variety of foliage typical of a tropical rainforest. The tops of the trees were softly blurred by the mist, adding to the tranquil and slightly mysterious ambiance of the scene.

Overall, the view from the Paluma Dam captured the quiet beauty of a rainforest in the midst of a rainy or misty day, with a sense of peaceful isolation from the rest of the world.

I would walk further up the track to the west. The track itself was a dirt path, damp from the rain, leading deeper into the forest toward the old *Eucalyptus grandis* trees and the fork with the long road to Jourama on the right, and the old gate with its vast network of trails and lookouts beyond. The path was flanked on one side by a line of large rocks, providing a barrier or demarcation. The trees here were tall and dense, with slender trunks and lush green foliage, typical of the rainforest environment in the area. The forest floor was covered with leaves, twigs, and other natural debris, adding to the wild and untouched feel of the place.

At the end of the day, we knew the rain wasn't going to relent for the next few days, let alone hours. Realising that staying would be impractical and possibly unsafe, we made the decision to pack up and head back down the mountain. The dense clouds continued to wrestle with the rainforest canopy, pouring down heavy rains that seemed determined to wash everything clean for the coming new year.

Turning around, however, showed something less stellar. The foreground showed a patch of grass that was wet from the rain, with water pooling in certain areas. Just beyond the grass was a low retaining wall made of interlocking blocks, likely intended to prevent erosion or provide some structural support.

On top of the wall, there was a gravel-covered area with several tall trees standing close together. The rain had darkened the tree trunks, and the foliage was thick, creating a lush canopy. There were also several black bollards or posts lined up along the edge of the gravel area which could be barriers to prevent vehicles from entering the region beyond them.

In the background, there was a green-roofed shelter, likely a picnic shelter, with a few wooden picnic tables underneath it. The shelter was partially obscured by the surrounding trees and appeared to be a place where visitors could take cover from the rain. The entire scene was damp and misty, with the rain adding a sense of calm and seclusion to the area. The overall atmosphere was serene, but also somewhat isolated due to the heavy rainfall. Looking around, the camping ground's only remaining inhabitants seemed to be the dark bollards that lined the dirt path.

We weren't the only ones making the decision to retreat; many other campers and visitors, including our friend Paco Parigi, also chose to leave. Paco, a fellow seasoned sailor, looked like he'd been through a storm at sea, despite not even setting foot on the water. His campsite, when we visited during a brief lull in the rain, was a scene of chaos, mud everywhere, tents soaked through, and gear scattered about like remnants of a battlefield. It was clear that the weather had turned what was meant to be a peaceful retreat into a challenging and muddy ordeal.

As we made our descent, the natural beauty of Paluma's landscape provided a stunning backdrop to our retreat. The waterfalls, usually a tranquil flow, had been transformed by the continuous downpour into powerful cascades of crystal-clear water. They streamed down the rocky cliffs in magnificent sheets and ribbons, creating a breathtaking spectacle. The sight was a reminder of the raw and untamed beauty of nature, even in less-than-ideal conditions.

While it was disappointing that we couldn't stay and enjoy the weekend as planned, the adventure of navigating through the rain-soaked wilderness and the mateship among the group made it a memorable day.

Little did we realise at the time that this relentless storm was merely a prelude to something far greater. The torrents of water pouring from the sky were not just a passing inconvenience; they were the beginnings of a much larger event. As the rain continued unabated, all this water would eventually gather and flow together, culminating in a great flood. Looking back, it almost felt like a prophecy of fantasy fiction being fulfilled, a forewarning of both the devastation that was to come and the stories of resilience and heroism that would emerge in its wake. This flood would test the strength and spirit of the community, and while it brought challenges, it also paved the way for acts of bravery and solidarity.

Chapter Six

The Surge in the Streets

I'm sure many people remember the torrential rainfall that led to the floods...

I must confess that, at first, I didn't think much of it. After all, I had just experienced a massive downpour up at Paluma myself. However, as the days progressed, it became clear that this was no ordinary storm. The rain didn't let up, and the rivers and streams began to swell. Then, the floods took form, rising steadily and ominously, transforming the landscape and reminding us all of nature's power. It was a turning point, one that caught many by surprise, including myself.

Before the official request to stay at home was issued, my mother and I took a drive around to observe the Ross River in full force before it became too dangerous. One of the first suburbs we visited was Railway Estate. I still remember seeing the roadsides swamped, with water breaching the driveways. We couldn't safely reach Rooney's Bridge, so we headed over to Bowen Road bridge instead. It was a confronting sight. The river had reached the very edge of its banks, and the water

A TIME FOR VOLUNTEERS

was roaring under the bridge. There was a footpath under that bridge that my friends and I had used for the Bloody Long Walk marathon, raising money for the Mito Foundation, in 2018. That was one of my fondest memories of that year, made more poignant by the lack of such events in Townsville since. It's still hard to believe how that footpath, along with many things along the riverbank, were now swallowed by water.

Afterwards, we drove to Mundingburra which was facing its own challenges. Trees had fallen, branches had snapped, and the roadsides were swamped. When we reached the playground next to the river, we could see that the water was raging and on the verge of breaching its banks. The rain was becoming so heavy that we had to call off our little observation drive. The reality of the situation was sinking in, and it was clear that this was more than just a typical heavy rain.

In the days that followed, those very suburbs would find themselves submerged under metres of water. The homes that once stood firm were torn apart; their inhabitants' lives irrevocably altered in a matter of days. The flooding reshaped the landscape, leaving communities to face an uncertain future as they began the arduous process of recovery and rebuilding. The devastation was swift and indiscriminate, affecting everyone in its path and forever changing the lives of those who called these neighbourhoods home.

You bet that after the whole debacle I heard people complain hard about the new suburbs being built on unstable, flood-prone ground around the Ross. Truthfully, I have nothing new to offer there. I aim to detail my experience, not change the entire system.

As I watched the news unfold on television that day, the scenes of the State Emergency Service and dedicated volunteers working tirelessly to combat the rising waters struck me deeply. In the suburb of Rosslea, residents hastily gathered their belongings, aware that the water levels were rapidly increasing with little warning. Some sought refuge on dry land or higher ground, while others prepared for the inevitability of being surrounded by water. However, in the face of this imminent danger, the comforting presence of helping hands was never far away. Strangers selflessly opened their homes to those in need, offering solace and support during this challenging time.

The scale of the evacuation efforts was immense. Hundreds of homes required evacuation, and emergency crews tirelessly assisted approximately 80 individuals in just one night. A firefighter testified to a reporter about the dire circumstances that had befallen the entire region. He acknowledged the significant assistance that had arrived from Brisbane, demonstrating the unity and collaboration of emergency response teams in times of crisis. An SES volunteer, as he navigated the floodwaters on his boat alongside the reporter, shared his astonishment at witnessing such an unprecedented event in Townsville. "It was definitely an eye-opener," he confessed with a slight chuckle, recognising the magnitude of the situation and the challenges it presented. The relentless downpour of the monsoonal rain continued unabated, further exacerbating the swelling of rivers and the subsequent flooding.

The resilience and determination displayed by the SES, volunteers, and the community at large during this time of crisis were truly remarkable. Their unwavering commitment to assisting and protecting those affected by the floods demonstrated the strength of the human spirit in the face of adversity. As the rivers continued to rise, and the deluge of rain persisted, the collective efforts of these dedicated individuals became even more crucial in mitigating the impact and providing support to the affected communities.

The Ross River Dam, now exceeding 200% capacity, presented a breathtaking sight as the floodgates were opened. The cascading water

A TIME FOR VOLUNTEERS 107

not only provided an awe-inspiring spectacle for onlookers but also served as a vital means of managing and storing the excessive rainfall. I vividly recall a particular moment from the news footage when two individuals, donning spray jackets, stood near the gushing flow and were unexpectedly sprayed by a small splash. The scene then shifted to a group of trees standing amidst the frothing river and a veil of silver mist, creating a hauntingly beautiful image.

The torrents of water pouring from the dam unleashed an unparalleled deluge upon the surrounding suburbs. In Oonoonba, street after street became inundated, forcing the evacuation of residents. Despite the unstoppable rampage of the floodwaters, the spirit of community remained resolute. Volunteers tirelessly filled sandbags, ensuring that anyone in need had access to this crucial defence against the encroaching water.

It was difficult to fathom the swift transformation that had occurred in just a week. Townsville had recently been under severe water restrictions due to drought conditions, and now the city found itself grappling with widespread flooding, an unprecedented weather event that most residents had never witnessed before. As authorities issued warnings of further flooding to come, the gravity of the situation intensified, and the uncertainty of what lay ahead weighed heavily on everyone's minds.

Throughout that day, the situation continued to evolve rapidly, with each passing hour bringing new challenges and developments.

Inside, our now late dog Bindii was having cabin fever, constantly wanting attention. A playful pup back then, the red cattle dog wanted to go outside and play around, like the energetic rascal she was. I'll remember that more fondly now. She'd grow up into a loving member of the family, who would always run up to greet you. During the writing of this book, on 20 August 2024, wanting pats more often and being less active, she was revealed to be masking pain from an aggressive cancer and had to leave this world a few months before turning six. She was my only companion when I had the house to myself, always in the corner of your eye and ear when she wasn't in front of you, now the silence in the front veranda will continue to be heavy.

On that fateful day, as the floodwaters reached their peak, my personal story unfolded. I embarked on a mission to capture and document the experiences of my own suburb with as much detail as possible. While the severity of the flooding in my area may not have been as severe as in others, there were still moments etched in my memory that I will never forget.

It started in Stanton Terrace, a charming street in the suburb of North Ward. The location offers breathtaking views of the entire neighbourhood and the prominent Castle Hill, which majestically presides over our community. Anyone familiar with the front of Castle Hill would recognise the large, rocky slope that stretches from its summit to its middle. During the summer monsoon season, it's not uncommon to witness a few cascading waterfalls adorning this slope. Observing those delicate white ribbons flowing down the hillside has always been a delightful sign for me. It signifies that our region has received its fair share of rain, evoking a sense of joy and anticipation. It signals that it's going to be a good day.

That was certainly not the case when, on the 3rd of February, I bore witness to a powerful sight. The waterfalls this year were unlike anything I had seen before. Two massive streams of water, reminiscent of gracelessly folded white curtains, descended the stone wall. Even before reaching the base, these streams merged and united into an even more formidable torrent. I could observe the very end of the waterfall where it flowed through the spaces between my neighbours' properties. The intensity and volume of the rushing water were unlike anything I had ever witnessed before. It was a force of nature in its full glory.

As I stood there, capturing the awe-inspiring scene before me, I couldn't help but feel a mix of astonishment, reverence, and concern. The sheer power of the water's flow served as a poignant reminder of the formidable forces of nature and their capacity to reshape the world around us. Little did I know then that this was just the beginning of the flood's impact on my suburb and the unfolding events that would shape my personal flood story.

Continuing my exploration, I followed the path of the water as it flowed down the large-diameter drain, which eventually opened into a narrow by-way adjacent to Stanton Terrace. As I descended towards the by-way, a thunderous roar greeted my ears as the water rushed out of the drain with remarkable force, reminiscent of an express train hurtling down the tracks. It then plunged into another drain beneath the road. The immense volume of water had been channelled and concentrated into this small tunnel, creating a striking analogy to how light can be focused into a laser beam.

A similar scene unfolded near the smaller storm drain at the top of the street's incline. The white, frothing waters surged out of the tunnel, crashing against the stone barriers that struggled to contain their fury. It was a mesmerizing and somewhat unsettling sight. And yet, this was just one of the many waterfalls that appeared in unexpected places, transforming familiar surroundings into a spectacle of nature's raw power and unpredictability.

Moving further along the street, the situation remained dire. The hillside wall boasted yet another small waterfall, accompanied by a fallen rock that had come loose from the cliff face. Astute council workers had promptly placed traffic cones near the fallen rock, one of which sat atop it like a funny hat. The rock has since been nudged back into the vegetation.

Approaching the end of that section of the street, I was met with another tumultuous intersection of storm drains where an uncontrolled torrent raged. The scene resembled the spillway at Paluma Dam's reservoir, devoid of the usual signs of amphibian life breeding there. Just a few dozen metres further, I glanced up at the cliff face, only to witness more waterfalls cascading down like alien invaders. The sheer amount of water that had accumulated on the hill was astounding. How long would this downpour continue? How would the landscape be forever altered?

I walked on, eventually reaching the top of the hill that divides the Terrace in two, where I could see Castle Hill shrouded in mist and heavy rain. The hill's rugged slopes were partially obscured by low clouds. The rain and mist gave the vegetation on the hill and the trees in the foreground a lush, vibrant green appearance. Several homes were nestled at the base of the hill with their modern architecture contrasting against the natural landscape. The visibility was reduced due to the thick fog, emphasising the intensity of the weather and the hill's imposing presence.

As the tiny mountain loomed, hidden within the ghostly grey clouds and mist, a profound realisation washed over me. This was not just a mere flood; it was a natural disaster teetering on the edge of catastrophe. It would become a tale spoken of for years, recounted at social gatherings and chronicled in news articles. If our community were to recover from this devastating event, we would need to come together, united in our efforts. I knew in that moment that I had to join forces with my friends and volunteer. The sight of the unfolding disaster had solidified my resolve. It was clear that the path to recovery would require collective action.

Continuing my walk, I made my way towards Stanley Street where I encountered more intriguing sights amidst the floodwaters. Queen Street was a small road that intersected with Stanley Street; I had taken that left turn walking the dog countless times, and I'll remember moments like these when it had transformed into a watery passageway. On both sides of the road, there were curved white concrete barriers, partially submerged, indicating that this is a low-lying area prone to flooding. Surrounded by vibrant greenery, it presented a whimsical and somewhat comical scene.

The water flowed from a higher point to a lower area, creating a small waterfall effect over the edge of the road, demonstrating the force of the water. The water appeared to be brownish, likely due to sediment and debris carried by the floodwaters.

It was as if the residents knew the water would inevitably flow through their street, so they embraced it by turning it into a decorative feature, a light-hearted touch in the midst of the chaos.

As I turned my attention to the drain flowing beneath Stanley Street, I couldn't help but marvel at the ingenuity of the engineers who had designed this system of storm drainage. Their foresight was remarkable, as the water, despite its immense destructive potential, flowed through the drain with minimal damage. Above, Castle Hill loomed, its white waterfall cascading ominously, serving as a constant reminder of the powerful forces at play.

Returning to Stanton Terrace, I observed water flowing down areas where I used to play as a five-year-old. I imagined my younger self finding joy in such a scene, much like the whimsicality of Queen Street. The water flowed smoothly, creating a serene and peaceful ambiance amidst the storm's chaos. In the midst of the devastation, it was comforting to witness pockets of beauty and tranquillity, serving as a reminder that even in the darkest times, there can be moments of solace and respite.

These pleasant sights amidst the storm offered a glimpse of hope and reminded me of the resilience and capacity for finding joy even in the face of adversity. I would revisit these places walking the dog, and will walk them still.

As I settled back into the comfort of my dry and warm house, the sound of rainfall persisted, tapping rhythmically on the tin roof, while the winds continued their relentless howling outside. Amidst this soundscape, a new noise cut through the air, an unmistakable thumping that could only belong to an army helicopter. It was a rare sight to behold, considering the grey that had dominated the sky for days. Intrigued, I decided to investigate further.

I turned to FlightRadar24, an online flight tracking service, to see if any flights to Townsville had been impacted by the inclement weather. To my surprise, there were none. The airport had been closed due to the prevailing conditions. However, what I did observe on the radar were a pair of MRH-90 Taipan helicopters, belonging to the Army's 5th Aviation Regiment. They had departed from Townsville at 5:59PM to an unknown destination with a highlighted flight path tracing along the coastline at 550 feet and slowly descending, before heading inland. The lead chopper, Registration A40-011, was identified as "HSLR11," likely translating to "Hustler 1-1," which was one of their radio call signs. I was fortunate enough to capture a photograph of this remarkable sight.

Reflecting on this encounter, I couldn't help but feel a profound sense of respect and admiration for the skilled pilots who dared to navigate helicopters in such treacherous weather conditions. The level of expertise required to manoeuvre aircraft under these circumstances was immense. I acknowledged the courage and capability demonstrated by these pilots, whose unwavering dedication to their duty and the safety of others was truly commendable.

Darkness did not bring peace in this troubling time. The rain kept on pouring and pouring. It was absolutely relentless, just never stopping. My house's tin roof sounded like it was being sprayed by a fire engine. My home felt more like a ship than a house, riding the rough seas through the gale. It reminded me of that episode of *The Goodies* when they were maintaining a lighthouse during a rough storm and the lamp burst, forcing them to get comically creative to warn the incoming ships. Yes, that was my honest analogy for that time. The late Tim Brooke-Taylor's performance of panicked shouting and whimpering was especially memorable then. His passing later on only made this moment more of a special memory. He will be remembered by me, and many others.

The relentless downpour of rain during the flood brought forth vivid memories of another powerful natural disaster: Cyclone Yasi. It was during that time that we found ourselves confined to our homes, besieged by the intense rain. Our main focus was ensuring the structural integrity of our house while fervently hoping for the safety and well-being of our loved ones.

I remember the morning well. The memory being especially vivid during Kirrily. My father and I went out briefly in 2011, and I saw several households boarded up. On the way back was a CH-47 Chinook carrying a load in its sling. The first clouds at the edge of the cyclone crept across the sky over the ocean, like a mothership in an alien invasion story. The wind was gentle but not embracing. Chilling, but not comforting. The calm before the storm, rising among the forming clouds all around. Aside from wind, there was not a sound as we all waited for the fall. Then the rain came, and Magnetic Island disappeared into the grey. The winds began to sing, first quite low, then loud, and at last with a deafening chorus. The night fell, giving way to a continuous, thunderous roar. I still do not know how I had found sleep during that.

The following day, as the remnants of Cyclone Yasi began to dissipate, I ventured outside to witness the aftermath in my suburb. The scene that unfolded before me was one of devastation. The once-majestic trees on the hill had been torn asunder, their branches scattered and broken. Even the great towering trees that provided shade in Queens Gardens had been battered by the cyclone's ferocity. They were stripped down like a carcass, yet they stood, refusing to be brought down. The rest of the trees continued to endure a battering, flowing like coral in the sea. The bougainvillea in our garden wall gave way, falling on the swing set. The water glazed the balcony as the trees swung wildly. More than once, I thought they were going to fall. Then there was the storm tide, with waves crashing into and over the breakwater wall. In my grandmother's house, a small tree couldn't take it anymore and broke. The wilderness beyond was even worse, looking like a barren warzone in every view, to say nothing of the driveways and streets full of debris. The sun shining for a brief moment brought even more detail to it all.

Looking back on the photos showed more moments of that day. Like a beached yacht and a tree that fell, uprooted, and lifted up a Mitsubishi truck that was parked next to it. In Cardwell, there was the image of all kinds of pleasure boats piled up and crammed together in the side of the breakwater like a scrapyard, and the oceanside area razed and covered in sand with some slabs of the road upheaved. The imagery of palm trees pulled in one direction from the wind was seen everywhere, as was the crashing of brown water surf. That was a sight on the beaches of Townsville. The Pallarenda baths where Dad and I would go had been torn apart. The storm's fury was seen in full

A TIME FOR VOLUNTEERS 115

force at the Strand, with violent sea spray in the water, entire tree branches scattered on the pathway, the wind turbine collapsed. It was a similar sight all across the city, with trees of all species falling on their side like wounded giants. An image of Charters Towers' Mylonas Building was also archived, as was another place in Tully. Caravan parks were nasty sights, with entire caravans upside down and smaller debris everywhere.

The rest of the town shared in the harrowing aftermath of the storm's wrath, and in the moment of 2019, I couldn't help but feel a sense of trepidation, hoping that this flood wouldn't leave a similar path of destruction in its wake.

Cardwell, in particular, bore the wrath of Yasi...

In August 2022, I stayed there during the break week of my semester; A peaceful, slow-paced getaway. The kind of town just small enough that you can see the whole thing in a day, but quiet enough that you can sleep in and not miss much. Exactly what I was after. Under the warm tropical sun, I strolled the main road, visited the Cardwell Bush Telegraph Museum, and soaked in the history through the lens of the locals themselves.

One section of the museum was dedicated to Cyclone Yasi, the defining event that the town will always be remembered for. The storm surge reached seven metres, devastating 75 per cent of Cardwell's buildings. The Port Hinchinbrook Marina was destroyed, 150 vessels heaped together in a chaotic tangle that would become one of the most infamous images of the disaster.

But more powerful than the photos were the stories. Local voices captured in their own words, describing the sound of the wind screaming through the town a full hour before Yasi struck, like being trapped beneath a wooden railway bridge as fifty freight trains thundered by. When the storm passed, the place they called home was unrecognisable.

Now, if this were some speculative fiction story, which I've written about a lot, Cardwell would've remained a destroyed town turned post-apocalyptic wasteland, maybe with some *Walking Dead* or *Mad Max* story of survivors thrown in. Fortunately, the real world is mostly different from that, so the people of Cardwell saw the mess before them and rolled up their sleeves. They didn't wait for someone else to fix it. They helped each other. They set aside differences. They dug deep and did what needed to be done. The town's story became one of strength and shared purpose, of mateship in the truest sense.

Some locals were even treated to the Yasi Recovery Concert in Townsville, one small gesture to honour their ordeal. But perhaps the biggest takeaway from that time was a changed perspective: how fleeting life can be, how important it is to look after one another, and how powerful community can be in the face of catastrophe.

As the saying goes… Life isn't about waiting for the storm to pass. It's about learning to dance in the rain. Cardwell had done just that.

As night fell in 2024 during Cyclone Kirrily, it was a similar feeling brought on by escalation. The wind was roaring. The trees were shaking and groaning louder than ever. There would usually be a few moments when it was gradually rough, followed by an even more powerful squall.

The scene outside was chaotic. The wind howled through the trees, bending their trunks and whipping their branches with a ferocity that seemed unending. The noise was a constant roar, punctuated by the occasional crash as branches snapped. Then, around 10 PM, the wind gradually died down. Eventually, it came to a stop, more or less. The rain seemed to disappear earlier, too. We were in the eye. Cyclone Kirrily didn't have a tightly formed eye, but rather it was wide and clear. Stepping outside during this brief reprieve was surreal. The sky, once a swirling mass of dark clouds, now revealed a few stars peeking through. The air was still, almost eerie in its calmness, a stark contrast to the tumultuous hours we had just endured. It felt like standing in the centre of a massive, quiet void, with the promise of the storm's return hanging heavily in the air.

In both instances, darkness covered the sky and the ground for the first time in a long time. We were like this for at least two nights in 2011, and three in 2024. Only the lights of the occasional car down Gregory Street cast an artificial sort of light. My unique, neurodivergent mind still had imaginary friends back in 2011, and I went down another journey in the land of imagination where we were a force of light comprised of humans, animals and aliens, taking to the skies in science-fiction planes and defeating the aliens that represented the cyclone. It was a fun trip in my mind, and those little adventures inspired me to write later on. If I were not charging my phone in 2024, I would have surely listened to some more of Roger Whittaker's music like I did back on those nights. His *Mexican Whistler* song, which has melodic whistling accompanying the acoustic guitar instead of vocals, was so delightful in that moment. His music in general stands out to me.

Fortunately, in comparison to both cyclones, the next morning of 2019 brought a sense of relief as the rain eased, and the floodwaters receded in our immediate vicinity. However, the suburbs on the other side of the hill painted a different story. The impact of the floodwaters had taken a toll on those areas, and the challenges faced by the residents there were yet to be fully understood...

Chapter Seven

By First Light

In reflecting upon the various chapters of my life, including the transformative experiences of globetrotting and volunteering, a profound realisation has dawned upon me: Individually, we are mere drops, singular entities traversing the vast canvas of existence. However, it is in the collective memory of shared moments, endeavours, and challenges, such as the Townsville Floods, that we coalesce into a formidable force, akin to the expanse of an ocean. These events stand as poignant reminders that our strength lies not solely in our individual capacities but in the unity that emerges when diverse drops converge, creating a force greater than the sum of its parts. Together, we become an ocean, capable of surmounting obstacles, shaping destinies, and leaving an indelible mark on the canvas of humanity.

Back to 2019, the following day brought further events that unfolded amidst the ongoing flood crisis.

Taking a step back to examine the broader picture, the entire Townsville flood was instigated by a slow-moving tropical low, situated northeast of Mount Isa. This low-pressure system became embedded within a stalled but highly active monsoon trough. The convergence of northerly, moisture-rich monsoonal air from the tropical low and coastal south-easterly winds created a zone of atmospheric instability. As a result, the combined air masses were driven westward over the mainland. This weather system persisted for approximately one week, remaining relatively stationary and generating consistent medium to heavy rainfall across the affected areas. Intermittent heavy showers and locally damaging winds also occurred, contributing to the overall impact.

Truly extraordinary circumstances presented an unusual set of conditions, ultimately leading to major to historic flooding across the Townsville region. The convergence zone created by the opposing air masses, combined with the prolonged period of rainfall, resulted in the overwhelming inundation experienced by the community. The persistent nature of the system, with minimal deviation or movement, exacerbated the intensity and duration of the rainfall, leaving the region grappling with the severe consequences of widespread flooding.

The magnitude of the flooding and its extensive impact on the Townsville area can be attributed to the unique combination of meteorological factors at play. As the community confronted the immense challenges posed by this exceptional weather event, it became evident that this was no ordinary flood but a historic event that would leave a lasting mark on the region's collective memory.

The memories of the devastating Brisbane floods in 2010 and 2011 were still fresh in my mind as I witnessed the unfolding disaster in Townsville. Those floods, which rank among the most catastrophic in recent Australian history, claimed the lives of thirty-five individuals and impacted over two hundred thousand people. The Brisbane floods were not a singular event but rather a series of floods brought on by severe weather conditions in the preceding months.

In both the Brisbane floods and the 2019 Townsville floods, the Australian Defence Force swiftly mobilised to provide assistance to those affected, and volunteers from across the country joined forces to lend a helping hand. Brisbane had faced flooding in the past, most notably in 1974 when the riverbanks breached, causing widespread devastation. Witnessing a similar disaster unfold in my own city was a disheartening experience. Although I acknowledged that the scale of the Brisbane floods was much larger and wider than the floods in Townsville, the sight of entire neighbourhoods being submerged in water was nonetheless distressing.

The impact of the 2011 floods in Brisbane reached far beyond its immediate vicinity. Many Townsville residents, myself included, had friends and family members residing in Brisbane, adding a personal connection to the disaster. At 11:00AM on a Monday, I distinctly remember my high school holding a moment of silence for Jordan Lucas Rice, a brave young boy who tragically lost his life during the floods. He selflessly insisted that his younger brother be saved before him, and his heroic sacrifice, along with that of his mother, will forever be remembered. In 2015, Jordan was posthumously awarded the Australian Bravery Medal in recognition of his courage.

During the Brisbane floods, a strong volunteer spirit emerged, with over 55,000 registered volunteers stepping up to assist in cleaning up the streets, and thousands more donning gumboots and armed with mops to lend a hand. The Prime Minister at the time praised the tremendous Australian spirit demonstrated through the collective volunteering effort, highlighting the resilience and unity that permeated throughout Queensland. The catchphrase "If it's flooded, forget it" became a powerful reminder of the dangers associated with flooded vehicles, a lesson that should never be forgotten. The experiences of the Brisbane floods served as a poignant reminder of the devastating power of nature and the resilience of communities in the face of adversity. The spirit of volunteerism that emerged during those challenging times exemplified the strength and compassion of the Australian people.

Going back to 2019, as news continued to pour in about the fateful night when the Ross River engulfed Townsville, the extent of the flood damage became chillingly evident through aerial footage that captured the aftermath in harrowing detail. The recorded rainfall totals during that time surpassed even the infamous 1998 "Night of Noah," establishing it as one of the most severe flood events in the region's history.

With the Ross River Dam gates fully open, an astonishing two million litres of water surged through the city every second, inundating streets and homes. The scale of the devastation was staggering, with more than twenty suburbs submerged by the rising waters. As the crisis unfolded, reports emerged of crocodiles being spotted in the streets, a stark reminder of the unprecedented nature of the flooding.

Evacuation centres quickly reached capacity, prompting the opening of additional centres to accommodate the overwhelming number of displaced residents. Tragically, over 100,000 people found themselves becoming refugees in their own city, seeking safety and shelter from the rising floodwaters. Entire neighbourhoods were transformed into makeshift shelters, with schools, community centres, and sports complexes repurposed to provide temporary refuge for those who had lost everything.

Amidst the chaos, there were stories of heroism and resilience. Two policemen found themselves trapped in their patrol car, their situation growing increasingly perilous as water levels continued to rise. Their plight mirrored that of countless others who urgently required assistance, underscoring the enormity of the task at hand. Rescue teams worked tirelessly, navigating treacherous conditions to reach those stranded by the floodwaters. Helicopters were dispatched for aerial rescues, and boats became lifelines for isolated residents.

Even in the face of such adversity, acts of courage and compassion shone through. Notably, members of the North Queensland Cowboys, local rugby league heroes, stepped forward to lend a helping hand. In the suburb of Fairfield, they transformed from sporting stars to rescuers, utilising their strength and skills to assist in the ongoing rescue and relief efforts. Their presence boosted morale and provided much needed support, embodying the community spirit that was vital during this time of crisis.

The flood had brought the community together, showcasing the indomitable spirit of resilience and unity. It was a time when ordinary individuals and notable figures alike put aside their differences and worked side by side, demonstrating the strength of the human spirit in the face of adversity. Volunteers from all walks of life came forward offering food, clothing, and shelter to those in need. Social media became a crucial tool for coordinating relief efforts, with residents using platforms to share information, request help, and organise aid distribution.

In response to the crisis, a remarkable force emerged: The Tinnie Army, a legion of Townsville citizens armed with their personal boats. The scale and impact of this extraordinary mobilisation were so remarkable that a more fitting term may be the Tinnie Armada. Historic footage captured the sight of an entire street filled with these resilient vessels, forming a small navy of aluminium, brimming with determined individuals. They served as worthy reinforcements to the hardworking boats of the State Emergency Service.

For those unfamiliar with the term, "tinnie" is an affectionate nickname for the small open aluminium boats which are a quintessential part of Queensland boating culture. These vessels are known for their durability, versatility, and ability to withstand years of fun and enjoyment. However, it's important not to confuse the term "tinnie" with its various other meanings, such as referring to beer cans in Australia, tinfoil in America, or... certain substances in New Zealand.

It is as they said during Cyclone Kirrily, "These names are just bizarre, aren't they? That's the big secret to the whole thing."

As the Tinnie Armada persevered, the community rallied together, united in their efforts to navigate the upheaval caused by the floods. Army vehicles traversed the waterlogged streets, while helicopters soared above, providing support and aid from the skies. Townsville Airport managed to reopen despite the challenges, serving as a crucial lifeline for supplies and personnel. Meanwhile, state schools remained closed, offering a unique learning experience for children who found themselves immersed in the realities of life in a disaster zone. This education, though unexpected, would undoubtedly prove valuable in shaping their understanding and resilience for future challenges.

The collective efforts of the Tinnie Army, alongside the numerous other individuals and organisations working tirelessly, exemplified the spirit of unity and mateship in the face of adversity. From the Army vehicles and choppers to the reopened airport and the dedicated educators, each person played a vital role in supporting and assisting the community as they navigated through the crisis. Their combined efforts showcased the unwavering strength and resilience of the Townsville community, leaving an indelible mark on the city's history.

The relentless force of the rivers and the persistent monsoon rains continued to wreak havoc, not only in Townsville, but also in the surrounding areas of Queensland. The devastating impact of the floods was not confined solely to the city but extended to the properties and communities across the region.

As the floodwaters surged, the properties and families located in the western parts of Queensland endured some of the most severe flash floods in recent memory. The once dusty plains and tranquil country bush, which served as their homes, transformed into a vast battlefield against the forces of nature. The Flinders River, normally a lifeline for these communities, turned into a ferocious torrent, swallowing road bridges and severing vital supply routes and transportation networks.

The consequences of these impassable roads and disrupted flow of supplies and people were far-reaching. The affected communities found themselves isolated and faced significant challenges in accessing essential resources and services. The resilience and resourcefulness of these communities was put to the test as they worked to overcome the obstacles posed by the flooded landscapes and limited connectivity.

Just as Townsville was grappling with the aftermath of the floods, the surrounding areas also witnessed the devastating power of nature as the monsoon rains unleashed their fury. The widespread battle against the floodwaters emphasised the impact and the urgent need for assistance and support throughout the region.

Graziers in the area had reported up to 300 millimetres of rain, and it was a similar sight for properties further out near Richmond. For those who had endured prolonged drought conditions, the arrival of the big wet was a welcome relief, although the shift from extreme dryness to intense rainfall presented its own challenges.

In the midst of this borderline war zone, the severity of the situation prompted the weather bureaus to issue a severe weather warning for the western regions. Unfortunately, four European tourists in Eddington, a small area off the Warrego Highway in the Shire of Murweh, found themselves caught off guard and learned about the warning the hard way. Thankfully, a local resident took swift action, using his Robinson helicopter to rescue their campervan from the rising floodwaters, showcasing the selflessness and community spirit in the face of adversity.

In Mount Isa, the local disaster management group was active and mobilised, working to ensure the safety and well-being of the community. Toll Aviation stepped in to rush supplies into the area, flying in fifteen tonnes of fresh produce to support the affected regions. The challenging conditions faced by the pilots and crew during these flights cannot be overstated as they manoeuvred through the enveloping grey clouds that seemed to stretch across the entire sky.

The news coverage also highlighted the resilience of property owners and locals who worked tirelessly to combat the floods. Toyota Landcruisers braved the muddy terrain with water creeping up to household doorsteps as they navigated through the challenging conditions. Property owners, driven by a sense of urgency, put in immense efforts to contain and mitigate the impact of the floodwaters.

Even the picturesque Prairie Creek, a place cherished by me and my friends for fond memories, was not spared, bursting its banks and adding to the overwhelming force of the floods. That creek, which cuts through the east of the town and the rural locality in the Shire of Flinders, is often passed by my close friend David and I on our way to Kooroorinya Races in May and the Prairie Races in August, the latter of which it is right next to. It was especially surprising news for me since I usually see that creek around the dry season where it often only bears dust.

As we drove past Castletown Shopping Centre along Woolcock Street later that day, we saw the entire lower carpark, once a bustling hub for shoppers, had been completely consumed by the floodwaters. Any cars that had been parked there were now surely submerged, adding to the growing list of casualties in this relentless deluge. The magnitude of the disaster was evident as we gazed upon the sunken vehicles, and the thought of salvaging them seemed like an arduous and formidable task, highlighting the extent of the challenges faced by the community.

At one point, in the confines of our car, the radio served as an image to the outside world, offering reports on the unfolding situation. The airwaves were abuzz with news that Coles, one of the major supermarket chains, had resorted to extraordinary measures, hiring a barge from down south. Desperate times indeed called for equally desperate measures, and the story was just one among many that the local radio stations relayed to listeners, both near and far. As they often do in cyclones and other natural disasters, these stations had become vital conduits of information, working tirelessly to keep the community informed and connected during these trying times.

And yet, it was essential to remember that the parts of the disaster I had witnessed were only a fraction of the larger picture. The flooding had touched countless lives, each with their own stories of resilience, loss, and recovery making the collective narrative of the disaster even more profound.

As we continued our journey, we found that even the lookout area at Castle Hill Road, a place where one could typically obtain a panoramic view of the city, was closed; A stark reminder of the challenges the region faced. Instead, the service track to the water tanks near Maidenhair Track offered an alternate viewpoint, providing a glimpse of the altered landscape and the resilience of the community against the backdrop of the flooding.

Confronted by the chaotic aftermath that had befallen my city during the Townsville Floods, a resolution stirred within me. The scenes of distress and upheaval became a call to action that resonated deeply, urging me to transcend the inertia of mere observation. Sitting idle was not an option when fellow community members were grappling with adversity. Uncertain of the precise nature of my role,

A TIME FOR VOLUNTEERS

I recognised that decisive action was imperative, action to meet the challenges unfolding today and those that would inevitably take form tomorrow. The only certainty was the imperative to volunteer, to contribute in whatever capacity the unfolding circumstances demanded. The call was clear, and with an unwavering commitment, I embarked on a journey to be of service, ready to adapt to the evolving needs of my community during this critical time.

People would have said such tasks were difficult or perhaps impossible. For some of the more naïve, that would be easy to say. The call of duty does not come from nowhere. Others have heard it before, from their own country, the home they served under. What should a volunteer carry out? An impossible task, knowing what it leads to? Even though it would be in the community's better interest?

Yes, those volunteers told us all with their actions. They should carry them out because it is only in the performing of them that they can prove to be impossible or not, but mostly not. How do you know they are impossible until you have tried them? If everyone said volunteering tasks were impossible to carry out when they were received, where would you be? Where would we all be if you just said impossible when orders came? I, for one, have seen enough of people, in high and low positions, to whom all orders were impossible.

In all the work that they, the volunteers, did, they brought added burden to themselves. For what? So that eventually there should be no more burden for others and so that the land should be a good place to live in. Was it difficult? Perhaps it was. But if they did not do it, many would still be dealing with the aftermath. No, there was nothing to be gained by leaving them alone.

It mattered not to me at that moment. The inner flame was burning with fury. Action was my only desire.

Perhaps the most troubling thing noticed during troubling times is the growing sense of despair, pessimism, and resignation if it is left to grow. It's as if people start to lose hope, convinced that there's no use in resisting, no point in striving for a better future. But I have to ask, is that really what we want? Are we ready to just surrender and accept our fate?

To anyone who thinks that I say this: No, absolutely not.

Yes, we've been hit hard. But the measure of our strength isn't about how hard we can strike back; it's about how hard we can be struck and still keep moving forward. That's what true resilience is all about. The darkness brought on by these floods is only temporary. It might linger for days, months, or even a year, but eventually, the pain will fade. If we choose to give up, though, that pain will never end, it will become a permanent part of our story.

We have to believe that things can change, that something better is possible. We could have chosen to stay down, to let this devastation consume us. But instead, we must choose to fight our way back into the light, to push forward against the odds. That's how we reclaim our future, and that's how we win.

So now I was in that mindset, my father and I had a decent task ahead of us one afternoon, one that we had been shouldering for years. For what felt like an age, we had been the stewards of Apple Lodge, a quaint property nestled on McIlwraith Street. Over the years, we had borne the weight of numerous responsibilities to keep the place in order. However, the recent deluge had presented us with an entirely new challenge.

As we stepped into the backyard, it was immediately apparent that the relentless rain had transformed the once familiar landscape into a soggy wilderness. The lodge's entire backyard and middle yard had been claimed by the rising waters, turning our serene haven into what could only be described as a tropical battleground. The lodge itself, with its weathered wooden exterior, now felt like a doomsday shelter, standing resolute in the midst of this watery onslaught.

Remarkably, the water had not quite reached the concrete step that marked the lodge's downstairs veranda, but it had come alarmingly close. The large tree that had been a central feature of the backyard was now marooned in the midst of this newfound marshland. The water, murky and unwelcoming, seemed to hold secrets beneath its surface, and one couldn't help but imagine something lurking in its depths. The whole situation was a stark reminder of the consequences of decisions made by builders of neighbouring developments. They had blocked crucial waterways, likely believing them to be superfluous. Well, the whole issue here speaks for itself, doesn't it?

Yet, as frustrating as this situation was, we found solace in the fact that, despite the chaos surrounding us, there was an odd sense of calm and peace in our transformed wetland. It was a stark contrast to the raging waters that had devastated other suburbs. Moreover, there was a silver lining, thin as it was, in the fact that the water had, for the most part, remained contained, sparing us from even greater damage.

We hitched an elaborate plan to get that water out. Being a sailor, my father had connections to the Townsville Yacht Club. He borrowed a siphoning device and a pair of large rubber hoses. We set a chair down in the middle of the pond and placed the siphoning motor on top of it, sticking out above the water. It would then drain the water through the tubes onto a pair of steel gutters and flow out the driveway. It was quite a resourceful scheme.

The majority of that afternoon was dedicated to a rather unglamorous yet crucial task - sitting by and supervising the hoses as they toiled to slowly drain the marshland that had overtaken our property. It wasn't an action-packed duty, but it was our frontline mission for the day, my post in the operation to reclaim our land from the watery invaders.

I was overseeing the draining process, while the sky above remained ominously overcast, casting a sombre and uncertain mood over the scene. It was during this time that I found solace in the audiobook of *Ghost Fleet* by P.W. Singer, a choice that was quite fitting. Much like the storyline in the book, where the United States reactivated its Navy reserve fleets as a low-tech contingency plan, we, too, were compelled to resurrect and employ old and improvised technology to confront an unprecedented and unexpected threat. As I sat in my chair, observing our backyard science experiment, the audiobook's narrative resonated with the situation at hand. We were working to turn the tide using unconventional methods in the face of a formidable adversary.

The reality of the situation was that this battle was not isolated to our property alone. The looming threat of the floods extended beyond our borders to the many other suburbs, each grappling with its own challenges. Railway Estate, in particular, served as a prime example. The rising waters had devoured the roads, leading to their closure by makeshift barricades. It was a stark reminder that the battle was raging not far from where I sat, and our struggle was mirrored in the efforts of communities throughout the region. We were all united in our drive to overcome this calamity and reclaim our lives from the relentless grip of the floodwaters.

The entire day unfolded like a scene from the aftermath, or perhaps even during the relentless rampage of a Kaiju, those giant mythical monsters often featured in franchises like *Godzilla*, *Pacific Rim*, and countless others that have captured the imagination of fans worldwide. It was ironic, really. I had always been a fan of those colossal creature features, the epic battles between larger-than-life monsters and humanity's ingenious efforts to counter them. But I had never envisioned myself thrust into a setting that mirrored those fantastical scenarios, although it had been the stuff of my dreams.

The glaring difference, of course, was the absence of an actual monstrous behemoth to serve as the epicentre of this unfolding event. Instead, the drama played out against the backdrop of a natural disaster, one that demanded just as much creativity and unconventional thinking to tackle effectively. It was a battle against the forces of nature, an entity far more formidable and relentless than any Kaiju that had ever graced the silver screen.

Ironically, 2019 had also seen the release of *Godzilla: King of the Monsters*, a movie that featured the villainous arch-nemesis, King Ghidorah, causing massive storms and wreaking havoc. It was eerie how the events of this storm debacle paralleled the actions of a fictional monster. The world had suddenly become a realm where the lines between reality and cinematic fantasy blurred, where nature's wrath felt like a manifestation of monstrous intent.

In all these narratives, there was a recurring theme that resonated deeply with the situation at hand; the arrogance of humanity in thinking that we could control nature, rather than acknowledging that the balance of power often tipped the other way. Our endeavours to combat the floodwaters, much like the attempts to defeat Kaiju in the movies, reflected the stark reality that nature was an uncontrollable force, reminding us of our place in the grand scheme of things. It was a humbling lesson, a reminder that, at times, we are mere spectators in the epic drama of our own planet, subject to the whims of a force far greater than any fictional monster.

As the grey day gradually transitioned into dark dusk, we had managed to make some headway in draining the lawn, and the once-flooded landscape had been largely cleared. The chair I had occupied for most of the day now sat amidst small puddles in the mud, mirroring the sepia reflections of nearby lights that painted a subdued, otherworldly atmosphere. With our immediate task completed, it was time to pack up our equipment and head back home.

Our journey home was a quiet one, and it wasn't long before we settled in for a much-needed night's rest, well aware that the next day would bring with it another round of challenges and, perhaps, another big adventure.

The following morning, I made my way to the Yacht Club to return the syphoning equipment, and then I decided to take a detour to check on the progress at Apple Lodge. What I encountered was disheartening. The swamp on the lawn had resurged, reclaiming the territory we had fought so hard to drain the previous afternoon. It was a frustrating setback, one that signalled the impending challenges of the days ahead. It was clear that this was going to be a long and arduous week.

As we grappled with our own difficulties, news from other suburbs continued to filter in. Makeshift shelters were being set up to provide refuge for the victims of the floods. Interviews with these brave individuals revealed a resilience that was nothing short of inspiring. Many of them had not lost hope or their sense of pride, even in the face of such adversity. However, the anguish of losing their homes was an ever-present shadow, a painful reminder of the hardships they were enduring.

It was during moments like these that the stark contrast between our circumstances and those of the flood victims became painfully apparent. Being safely ensconced in my home, far removed from the chaos and suffering, felt uncomfortable. There was a deep-seated need to be part of the solution, to channel my resources into making a difference for those still struggling. This was the driving force behind my decision to volunteer, a choice to stand in solidarity with those in need and contribute in any way I could to alleviate their hardships.

Returning home from that long day, I decided to take a moment to sift through social media, eager to gain insight into the floods from the perspectives of others. What I encountered were a plethora of videos and images that provided a firsthand account of the devastation and chaos unfolding in people's lives.

These visuals captured the grim reality of the situation. Homes overtaken by murky floodwaters, entire streets replaced by vast expanses of water, and balconies offering a bleak panorama of the inundated landscape. It was a sight so terrible that words seemed inadequate to describe the gravity of the flooding. The inundation was pervasive, affecting nearly every corner of the region, leaving a trail of destruction in its wake.

Amidst this digital flood of shared experiences, I distinctly recall coming across a post by MP Scott Stewart. In the video, he stood amidst the floodwaters, the water rising up to his knees, just outside his garage. With his usual articulate, solemn tone, he urged people to prioritise their safety during this trying time. His post also served as a vital reminder of the potential health risks associated with floodwaters, particularly the type contaminated with mud. It was a stark message that highlighted the immediate dangers and the importance of taking precautions in the face of adversity.

These social media posts were a window into the collective experience of the community, a medium through which we could share our struggles, extend support to one another, and raise awareness about the challenges that lay ahead. The flood had disrupted our lives, but it also fostered a sense of unity and resilience among those affected, reminding us that even in the darkest of times, the human spirit prevailed.

On another note… Help and support came from the outside world. I remember chatting with someone I know over social media – Rina

Hoshino, a Japanese American actress in Los Angeles. When she hoped I had a lovely weekend, I said "Well, my weekend was quite... eventful. My city is in a flood emergency right now. But it's under control now." Soon, Rina was looking into the news reports detailing the North Queensland situation and sent well wishes and support to us afterwards. So, word of the calamity was reaching international distances. I assured her that the lessons learned in Cyclone Yasi were proving useful here. Anything to help raise awareness was most appreciated. I returned the favour by raising awareness of her acting role as Mewtwo in *Detective Pikachu*.

As all of this was going on, the communities out west continued to be isolated, fighting their own battles. My Uncle Bartley would later share his experience, living in the rural locality of Basalt at the time, north of Charters Towers on the edge of the Burdekin River, in the vicinity of Fletcherview Research Station and the Gregory Highway. The water in the rivers surrounding his property had trapped him and the surrounding properties. It effectively turned them into an island near the Burdekin. He had no option but to sit back and ride it out, like many others. His property was indeed one of many facing such a situation. Uncle Bartley would always keep his cool when faced with such an event. You could've told him that this was coming in and he would say "Oh, that's not good, eh?"

All of that was my first day of volunteering, and through the dark grey clouds, a long week still lay ahead...

Chapter Eight

The Long Week of the Leviathan

In my many readings, I came across a Turkish proverb, *"He that falls by himself never cries."* I found it in the last chapter of *Shadow Command*, the 2008 addition to Dale Brown's *Patrick McLanahan* series. This simple yet profound saying speaks to the nature of personal responsibility and resilience. It suggests that when we encounter hardships or failures that are self-inflicted, there's an internal recognition that we are responsible for our own actions, and thus we do not seek pity or comfort. Instead, we face the consequences with stoicism and self-reliance.

The subsequent day unfolded with yet another formidable challenge, propelling me to a suburb still grappling with the lingering anguish caused by the Ross River's relentless breach. In the wake of the calamity, Townsville suburbs, notably Rosslea, Hermit Park, and Idalia, bore the brunt of major inundation. The torrential downpours, particularly in the northern enclave of Bluewater, led to perilous flash flooding. Record water levels at the Ross River Dam necessitated emergency measures, prompting the full opening of the dam's spillway, exacerbating the inundation downstream. The banks of the Ross River bore witness to severe erosion, inflicting structural damage upon pathways and boardwalks. One particularly hazardous section of the pathway succumbed to the relentless current, eroding supporting rocks and concrete, posing a significant threat to pedestrians. A pedestrian bridge near Aplins Weir suffered damage due to record spillway heights.

As news footage streamed in, it became evident that the emergency was far from abating. The water, unforgiving and unyielding, showed no signs of receding. A staggering two million litres per second continued to surge through the dam spillway into the Ross River, maintaining a peak level. The duration of this crest depended on the unpredictable trajectory of the weather system. The imperative remained clear: stay vigilant, stay home if possible, and remain tuned to authoritative messages. With over a thousand people still displaced and all five evacuation centres at capacity, the toll of exhaustion weighed heavily on the community. A weary populace settled in for yet another sleepless night, clinging to the hope that the relentless flow of support and resilience would eventually prevail against the formidable forces of nature.

Amidst the relentless fury of the Ross River, my cousin Darryl's family found themselves engulfed in the aftermath of the deluge. As the tempest subsided in Railway Estate, my family and I embarked on a mission to assist them in navigating the challenging situation that had befallen their home. Thankfully, being the owner of a quintessential Queenslander house, the flood's onslaught spared the crucial living spaces. However, the aftermath left an indelible mark on the property, turning the storage room, workshop, and laundry into disarray. The once pristine swimming pool and yard were now coated in a disconcerting layer of sludge. Our collective efforts were concentrated on the monumental task of emptying the storage room, a labour-intensive process that revealed the pervasive impact of the floodwaters. The items, once neatly stored, now bore the unmistakable imprint of mud and water, transforming the cleanup into a gritty endeavour that underscored the resilience required in the face of such natural calamities.

With a stockpile of unusable belongings in tow, we joined a formidable convoy of individuals, all sharing the common goal of heading to the dump. Our discarded items were welcomed without imposing any tip fees, providing a collective catharsis as we unloaded a myriad of items into the communal pile. Alongside Darryl, I tossed an array of articles into the heap, ranging from clothing to wood and even glass. Old relics, once cherished for sentimental value, met their demise, serving as a poignant farewell to products that had dutifully endured well past their prime. As the debris accumulated on our designated plot, a mirror I tossed into the mix shattered into pieces. Some might attribute it to years of purported bad luck, but I would rather make my own luck.

It was a good thing we went there to send our old stuff to Silicon Heaven when we did, as the line to release discarded possessions stretched beyond the gates, perhaps even extending further by the time our task was complete. The surging demand for disposal reflected the magnitude of the community's collective effort to cleanse homes and lives of the flood's aftermath.

The escalating demands eventually reached a crescendo, necessitating the establishment of a temporary dump in the Lou Litster Park, adjacent to Officeworks. This impromptu extension of disposal facilities became a testament to the community's adaptability and solidarity, as the flood's impact prompted swift responses and resourceful solutions to accommodate the needs of the many affected households.

In the ebb and flow of challenges, the collective spirit endured, transcending the confines of the conventional dump and extending to makeshift spaces like Lou Litster Park, where resilience manifested as a communal force capable of overcoming even the most unprecedented circumstances.

News kept coming through of the flooded areas. Now we were seeing crocodiles in trees. Oh, yes. They were sitting on the ones poking out of water, as swimming against the flow was proving too exhausting for them. That was some unsettlingly strange news. I thought if reptilian predators were learning to climb trees, we'd have a lot more to worry about in the future. I joked at the time that we would soon be seeing Drop Crocs emerge.

During the work in Railway Estate, I saw multiple Army vehicles roaming the street. These were the Bushmaster Protected Mobility Vehicles. We were in good hands with these big beasts coming to assist. For context, the Bushmaster is optimised for operations in northern Australia and could carry up to nine people, as well as equipment, fuel and supplies for three days. On the news, I could see one plough through the water, and another carrying a family to safety. These vehicles had already earned a name for themselves under Aussie, Dutch, and British service in Afghanistan, Iraq, and Syria. Now, though, they had come to help at home. Fortunately, the crews needn't worry about land mines here, just enormous washouts hidden by the water.

Even the ASLAVs (Australian Light Armoured Vehicles), eight-wheeled amphibious armoured reconnaissance vehicles, were being called to action. Footage and photos of them wading through the water were trending on social media and the news. Out of context, it would've looked like they were on a military operation in a foreign marshland. Instead, they were in the homeland, not even far from their barracks, coming to the aid of the civilians they were built to serve. The cavalry had literally arrived.

At a certain point during the chaotic events, a line of Bushmasters had parked near Darryl's street, lined up alongside the police forces, seemingly for a headcount or to coordinate their response efforts. It was a spectacle, akin to a parade of sorts, with Army personnel and police officers converging in a show of force. The gravity of the disaster had undoubtedly warranted the intervention of the Defence Force, and they had answered the call with full commitment.

I found myself among the curious and concerned civilians who had gathered on the sidelines, observing in awe the sight of these massive military machines rolling into the neighbourhood. The sense of reassurance that came with their presence was palpable.

During this gathering, I struck up a conversation with a blonde lady, likely a friend or neighbour of my cousin's family. As we conversed, our attention was drawn to a small helicopter navigating the turbulent skies. It was a striking image, a symbol of the relentless efforts to provide aid and support during these trying times. And it reminded me of the Taipan helicopters that had been a constant presence, flying through the challenging weather conditions.

It was heartening to see that the brave pilots of these helicopters received the recognition they deserved. Their mercy mission to the northwest had made it to the front page of the Townsville Bulletin, a well-deserved acknowledgment of their unwavering dedication. Flying through such treacherous weather conditions, they had exhibited exceptional courage and professionalism. To honour their remarkable story, the newspaper had arranged a photo with pilots Lieutenant Mathew Cupitt and Captain Brett Morrissey in front of the Taipan helicopter that had transported essential supplies, including fodder and aviation fuel, to the flood-stricken farmers in Cloncurry.

As of 2023, however, the Taipan has been retired early. While these helicopters had played vital roles in various operations, including providing crucial aid support during the Black Summer fires and multiple flood incidents, their early retirement became imminent due to a series of maintenance issues that had plagued the fleet. The torch has since been passed to the newer Black Hawk helicopters, signifying a changing of the guard in Australia's military aviation. The decision to retire the MRH-90 Taipan was further underscored by unfortunate incidents that unfolded in 2023. In March, during a training exercise, a mid-flight malfunction led to a controlled ditching over Jervis Bay. Later in July, during Exercise Talisman Sabre, a tragic crash occurred off the coast of Hamilton Island, resulting in the loss of four crew members. These unfortunate events confirmed the early end to their continued use.

The Australian Defence Force's swift and comprehensive response to the flood relief efforts certainly echoed their significant contribution to disaster response in the past. In 2011, the ADF launched Operation Queensland Flood Assist, establishing Joint Task Force 637, with its operational command centre based at Enoggera Barracks in Brisbane. This response was set in motion on New Year's Day of that year and marked a significant milestone in their history of disaster relief efforts. The deployment in 2011 was notably the largest for a natural disaster since Cyclone Tracy. The ADF's presence and support during that time were instrumental in aiding the affected communities and alleviating the suffering caused by the floods.

Eight years later, as I've described, they once again rose to the occasion and accomplished their mission in response to the flood disaster. The ADF's commitment to disaster relief and their dedication to supporting the community in times of crisis serves as a testament to their unwavering service and the vital role they play in ensuring the safety and well-being of the nation's citizens during times of calamity. Their tireless efforts in the face of these disasters continue to be a source of pride and reassurance for the Australian population.

More helicopter footage continued to air, portraying the city grappling with the biggest flood in living memory. We could all see the true devastation. There were still a lot of inundated houses, and probably maybe half of the Townsville community was flooded. The saturated landscape stretched from the north of Ingham to the south towards Ayr. Flooding was as far as the eye could see with suburb after suburb filled to the brim, and overflowing with destruction and heartbreak. Railway Estate, Hermit Park, and Rosslea were now unrecognisable, with Ross River Dam roaring through wide open gates. Supplies were on the way to communities still cut off more than a week on from the first downpours. But be it in the air or on the ground, it was the same heartbreaking story. How it would look tomorrow after the peak would only cause more pain.

Returning to my earlier mention of the 1998 "Night of Noah," for those unfamiliar with this significant event, here is a summary of the precursor to the recent floods. It all began with the remnants of ex-Cyclone Sid in the Coral Sea near Cardwell. This system generated a band of strong gales that gradually moved southward between Cardwell and Bowen. Wind gusts reached up to 90 km/h as it progressed into the Ingham area between 9pm and 9am on the morning of January 9th. During the day, the heaviest band of rain continued its southward journey, eventually reaching the Townsville area. Although Townsville experienced relatively light rain during the day, it was during the night that intense rainfall caused severe flash flooding and significant rises in stream and river levels. This event came to be known by its name as approximately 335 millimetres of rain fell on the 10th between 6pm and midnight, followed by an additional

236 millimetres in the next three hours. It is quite astounding, isn't it? Interestingly enough it was also the night my parents hosted over fifty friends for my first birthday party.

Late into the evening, the rain grew even heavier, reaching rates of 100 millimetres per hour, driven by strong gale-force winds. Since much of the city's terrain is relatively flat, the streets of Townsville quickly became submerged, obstructed by fallen trees and power lines. In certain areas, the water rose to three meters, inundating hundreds of businesses and homes in both Townsville and the then-separate Thuringowa. As a result, approximately 200 people had to be evacuated.

To the north, Black River suffered significant damage, with homes rendered uninhabitable, destroyed, or washed away as the river burst its banks. Bluewater also experienced substantial property damage, while in Townsville itself, five homes were destroyed, and hundreds more were flooded. The city faced widespread communication outages as phone services were disrupted in most areas. Fallen power lines and flooded substations resulted in power cuts affecting around 50% of households.

One notable impact in my family neighbourhood, Stanton Terrace, was the formation of a large washout that divided the street. Thankfully, our house and the cars left behind by our guests remained unharmed as we had an exit from our dead-end street. However, the gardens and driveways of houses on the downhill side of the street were severely affected.

Contrary to popular belief, there was no landslide that destroyed a million-dollar home on Stanton Terrace in 1998. The only landslide occurred in 2000 following Cyclone Tessi, and well after the initial disaster. The affected house happened to belong to my grandmother, although several neighbouring houses were also severely impacted. It is said that boulders were dislodged from Castle Hill and rolled down into Sturt Street in the CBD. If you examine the remaining boulders on the hill, you'll notice that some are held in place by steel ropes and cement. Additionally, a large rock and mesh wire wall has been erected to prevent further rockfalls.

Many similarities can be drawn between the 1998 and 2019 floods, with Townsville being declared a state of emergency on that fateful night. Numerous businesses remained closed due to the damage over the weekend, and the subsequent heavy rainfall forced a complete shutdown of the city. Many workers encountered renewed floodwaters in their attempts to return home, and even emergency responders had to halt their cleanup efforts for the remainder of the day. The period from the 10th to the 11th has since become known as the 'Night of Noah' among the residents of Townsville.

In light of this, I propose that we coin an equally colloquial, yet subtly biblical or mythological, nickname for the 2019 floods. Since my first writing of this, I've thought of some ideal candidates. Why not try... *The Weekend of Water, The Nights of Neptune, The Saturday of Scylla,* and my personal choice, the *Long Week of the Leviathan*. That particular one's got a catchiness to it, in my opinion. The whole disaster does feel quite like the rage of a sea monster making the deep boil like a pot. Minus, of course, the devouring fire from his mouth. I'm just saying that, on earth there is no other like this flood.

Over time, things began to wind down. But the floodwaters had left a trail of destruction in their wake. The time for rebuilding what was lost and gathering what still remained would soon be upon us...

Chapter Nine

The Rise of Team Townsville

As time passed, the devastating aftermath of the natural disaster began to recede into memory. The once ominous, rain-filled skies gradually cleared, and the warm, comforting sun returned to bless the land once more. The waters, once turbulent and destructive, started their slow but steady retreat, leaving behind traces of their destructive power. The scars etched into the landscape served as a constant reminder of the havoc that had been wreaked upon the community.

Many kept moving forward however they could, trying to return to normal or settle into a new normal. The sun still shone on the wet garden. The water in a stainless-steel mug was still cool and clean. The salty sea breeze from the Strand swayed the trees. I remember a performance of *Celtic Woman* was playing on the TV at one point, introducing me to my preferred genre for writing and calm time in general. Played upbeat, it can bring out joy for any occasion. Played slowly, it can soothe even the darkest night. With that, and other genres, I achieve perfect solitude, a state of mind where my writing is a well-oiled machine. In this world of being active and online at any given time, I find it important to return to the slower feeling, the present moment, however it can be interpreted.

Despite the gradual recovery, there were poignant reminders of the tragedy that still lingered. Houses, once homes to families, remained in various states of disrepair and ruin, bearing witness to the force of nature's fury. Overhead was the persistent presence of military helicopters, including the distinctive shape of the Boeing CH-47 Chinook, in the 5th Aviation Regiment's ongoing efforts to aid the afflicted and rebuild the shattered lives of the survivors. During my flight training in later years, I would fly alongside them, including the MRH-90 Taipans and the formidable Tiger ARH attack choppers. It was a surreal transformation, from witnessing the devastation from the ground to soaring above it.

Throughout this journey, I would meet up with my American friend, Jamie Lipsey. She had weathered the storm of our shared experiences, both the physical and emotional turmoil. Jamie, residing in the safe haven of Belgian Gardens during the floods, had escaped the watery grasp of the nearby creek. Our friendship deepened as we reconnected after the disaster, seeking solace in the routine of the gym where the memories of the floods were blissfully absent. Jamie had been with me through it all, from the initial shock to the arduous recovery, making the road forward feel less daunting with her unwavering support.

With the worst of the calamity behind us, my friend, David Hammer, and I decided to take a much-needed break. We embarked on a weekend getaway to Cairns, a respite from the trials and tribulations that had beset our city. Our itinerary was simple with a visit to the Australian Armour and Artillery Museum, followed by leisurely rounds of mini golf, and go-karting. As we settled in for an overnight stay at a backpacker's resort, we embraced the sense of escape that the weekend promised.

Yet, even in our temporary oasis, the echoes of our city's suffering were never far away. A chance encounter with the compassionate owner of an ice cream shop served as a poignant reminder of the collective grief that still hung over our community. After that, however, it was a nice sunny day of talking about the Bad Wolves' cover of *Zombie* in tribute to the late Dolores O'Riordan, as our friend Jarrod Towers was seeing them front for Nickelback at the time, and the then-upcoming *Avatar: The Way of Water*. Our return journey to Townsville was marked by scenic stops, including the beautiful Paronella Park, where nature's splendour clashed with the memories of a disaster.

The aftermath of the disaster had not extinguished the opportunities to extend a helping hand to those in need; if anything, they had only multiplied. The resilience and compassion of the community continued to shine brightly.

Various agencies had rallied together during the crisis, forming a united front against the destruction that had befallen the region. The State Emergency Service, the Queensland Government, and the Townsville City Council worked tirelessly alongside the Rural Fire Service, the Defence Force, and the dedicated volunteers of Team Rubicon Australia. Their combined efforts were a testament to the unwavering commitment to restoring normalcy to the lives of those affected. The local media had finally granted the Tinnie Army its name, which would be sealed in time for our own little brown-water navy.

My volunteering opportunity came in the form of Team Townsville. Recovering from a disaster was usually a gradual process. While in the comfort of my home, I got the recruitment email in my

A TIME FOR VOLUNTEERS 147

inbox, and I still have it archived today. It read: *"Safety is a primary issue, as are mental and physical wellbeing. If assistance is available, knowing how to access it makes the process faster and less stressful."*

To help people get back on their feet, Team Townsville, an initiative of Townsville City Council, Combined Churches, YWAM, and 99.9 Live FM was heading to the streets to care for the residents of Townsville by asking how they are and coordinating the connection of essential services to individuals and families. This was a unique opportunity to meet a huge need in our city, to look people in the eye and ask if they're okay.

Included in that email was another message, *"How are you going? R U OK? If you find you are struggling at this time – physically, financially, emotionally, or in any other way – and even if you're not, we encourage you to... reach out to friends, family, and neighbours for a chat, reach out to your church or club to connect, or contact Community Recovery and other services."*

Team Townsville's mission was clear... *"Working together to get Townsville back on its feet."*

As part of Team Townsville, our mission was clear: to support the recovery efforts in the areas of greatest need. We followed the lead of the State Emergency Service in addressing the highest priority areas, working methodically through the city according to the Council's designated priority zones. The impact we were making was profound, providing crucial assistance to individuals who had endured extremely traumatic circumstances.

To join Team Townsville, we first had to complete a one-hour orientation session where we learned about the organisation's vision and became familiar with the tools at our disposal to aid the community. I vividly recall attending one of these informative briefings at the

YWAM (Youth With A Mission) campus located in the heart of the CBD.

The plan was as intriguing as it was effective. We were grouped together, forming teams that would venture out to the neighbourhoods most affected by the disaster. Once in the field, these teams were further divided into pairs or small groups, each equipped with its own iPad. In addition, we carried leaflets containing emergency contact numbers vital for the ongoing recovery and aftermath of the floods. These iPads were not just for show; they played a crucial role in the process.

Our mission was straightforward yet impactful: we would approach residents and ask how they were coping in the aftermath of the disaster. This initial contact was an opportunity to connect with the affected individuals on a personal level, offering them a listening ear and a shoulder to lean on. But our assistance didn't stop there. The iPads served as tools for an optional survey which we could relay directly to the City Council.

Using these surveys, we could better understand the specific needs of each resident and assess how best to help them. Whether it was connecting them with essential services, arranging for necessary resources, or simply providing emotional support, we were committed to doing #whateverittakes to assist our fellow community members in their journey to recovery.

The hashtag "whateverittakes" became not just a slogan but a rallying cry for Team Townsville, embodying our determination to go above and beyond to help our community heal and rebuild. Funnily enough, that phrase would be a promotional quote in *Avengers: Endgame* later in the year. How perfect, I thought. It was time for the volunteers… to assemble.

I was ready to go instantly. This would be a terrific opportunity to help out in the aftermath. It involved walking, which was my favourite exercise, and working again with YWAM. Fortunately, I had just the right workwear for the job. I brought out my short sleeve work vest from my days on the medical ship in Papua New Guinea. Little did I know, however, that it wasn't going to be the only memory of Papua New Guinea that would be brought back.

I remember the first day: Wednesday, the 20th of February. After checking in at reception, I walked through the campus, which I hadn't seen for a while. It certainly brought back memories of the Wednesday night community barbecues of 2014. It also brought back the days of when my church group was there up until 2015 and again today. But those were in the past now. Today was a new day. A new generation. As Hemingway wrote, there is nothing else than now. There is neither yesterday, certainly, nor is there any tomorrow.

The whole crowd of volunteers was there, all packed and ready to go like it was an excursion or a bus tour. It was actually there that I met somebody from my days at the medical ship, Anna Scott. She was a leader then and now, as was her partner. Soon, it was time to head out. We all got aboard our Toyota HiAce vans which were also loaded with huge, barrel-sized water coolers. We were definitely going to need those. And then, once everyone was accounted for, we set off.

Our starting point was Lindsay Street in the suburb of Rosslea. Fittingly, the first suburb I arrived at was at the centre of the disaster. It made sense to start there. Rosslea is quite flat, sitting at approximately 5 meters above sea level. The eastern portion of the suburb is home to the Townsville Golf Club, while the remainder is primarily residential. Townsville Connection Road traverses the suburb from the south to the northwest. Due to its low-lying position near a river, Rosslea is unfortunately susceptible to flooding, particularly in the vicinity of the golf club.

As I walked down the street with my walking partner, a YWAM girl from New York State, we encountered some grim sights. Mud, dirt, tree bark, and rubbish were scattered everywhere. In some areas, it resembled a war zone. The waterline, marked by mud, was still visible and even at my height of six foot one, it was higher than me in some places.

Throughout the morning, we visited as many houses and units as we could. The people we met were still holding up with a strong sense of community spirit. However, it was clear that the experience had been painful for many. It was unfortunate that they had to endure such hardship. We hoped that the phone numbers we provided would help them on their path to recovery. As we continued, the extent of Rosslea's impact from the disaster became more apparent.

Our gathering spot for lunch was in Bicentennial Park at the carpark on Queens Road. The houses along that road had also suffered greatly during the floods, and it showed. Tree branches were piled up, and dirt and grass were strewn about. The Goodstart Early Learning centre on that road, which had been under repair for a long time after, looked as though it might have been lost. The lunch, provided by Subway, the Lions Club, and other volunteers, was a generous and noble gesture, much appreciated by everyone involved.

On Thursday, I was paired with an English girl and deployed around Diprose Street. It was at this point where things got really tough. Why? The heat. At this point, it was hitting a whopping 44 degrees Celsius. The mugginess was all around. On the bus we challenged ourselves to find what was the maximum safe UV rating. Several of us found that it was at the 11 point that you are not recommended to leave your house or go outside. But that day's UV rating? 13.3. With

A TIME FOR VOLUNTEERS 151

4 (or *Shi*, the number of death in Japan) and 13 (the ever-unlucky number for the West) popping up, unlucky numbers were hitting us left and right, and it sure felt so. To add more to it, I'm sure the temperature at some point was 108 degrees Fahrenheit for any North American readers.

Immense heat and comically exaggerated tetraphobia aside, we persisted and marched forward. We continued handing out numbers and filling out surveys.

However, the extreme heat caused our iPads to overheat. When they did, they displayed an error notification, closed the running survey program, and refused to start again until they were cooled down. Like any electronic device, iPads can overheat when their internal temperature exceeds a certain threshold. This triggers built-in safety measures to protect the device from damage which may include shutting down or closing applications to reduce heat generation.

It was my first encounter with this feature, but it was certainly better than the devices bursting into flames. The technology was giving up, but we certainly didn't.

The weather conditions during the current heat wave reminded me of the challenging climate I experienced during my time as a volunteer in Papua New Guinea. The scorching humidity, relentless storms, and demanding physical labour were a daily reality. Every day felt like an endurance test, pushing me to my limits.

But as I faced the intense heat and worked tirelessly, I couldn't help but feel a sense of gratitude for my previous experiences in Papua New Guinea. In that rugged and unforgiving environment, I learned the true value of resilience and the need to earn every small victory. The backcountry where we volunteered was a place where nature ruled, and survival depended on adapting and thriving amidst the challenges it presented.

It is important to acknowledge that while nature can indeed be awe-inspiring and beautiful, it can also be unforgiving and harsh. The romanticised notion of harmonising with nature without understanding its true complexities can lead to dangerous situations and misconceptions. Mother Nature does not follow human ideals or have a singular treatment for everything

A lot of people I've met in my urban bubble tell me that Mother Nature is wise, pure, and has a treatment for everything. Some have never learned the real rules, so they think they can just make up their own. They idealise the natural world, thinking that connecting with it brings out the best in you.

For instance, venturing into the PNG rainforest with the intention of being "one with nature" without proper preparation and knowledge can have severe consequences. The rainforest is a challenging and diverse environment where potential threats like malaria, dehydration, sunstroke, and various infections lurk. Such a victim would've wanted to harmonise with nature before they realised, too late, that nature is anything but harmonious.

I vividly remember the time when I was in Papua New Guinea and I experienced a large red swelling on my face. The Medical Officer speculated that it was an insect bite, but I couldn't even recall when I received it. To my astonishment, the swelling grew to such an extent that it altered the appearance of my right upper cheek. It was a stark reminder of the unpredictable nature of the environment I was in, and the potential risks associated with it.

Despite the challenges I encountered, I found myself appreciating even the toughest moments. Crushing my finger under the weight of a loaded oil drum while loading it into a scorching hot storage compartment, waking up early for deck watch, and navigating a boat through rough seas became part of my daily routine. These experiences

A TIME FOR VOLUNTEERS 153

tested my resilience and taught me valuable lessons about perseverance and adaptability.

I must also mention the senior deck officer again. His strict approach was necessary, considering the immense responsibilities and vast experience he carried as a part of the merchant navy. I understood that his demanding nature was a result of prioritising safety and maintaining high standards.

But I still recommend it. It should have been that way indeed. I grew from it and was hardened against similar climatic hardships. I vowed to never complain about the heat or rain ever again. It was a hard slap to reality that I needed. If it didn't challenge me, it wouldn't have changed me.

At home, I honestly find it difficult to talk to people about it. You would be surprised how easy some of them disregard it as just my experience, or just simply being in Papua New Guinea. They don't notice my discontent when they do that.

As we saw with the floods, Mother Nature is a malevolent witch at times. She's cold, unsympathetic and doesn't care about your spirit or your spoils. She only cares to impose a world where only the strongest and swiftest survive... and those who are most adaptive to change live in the long run...

But I digress...

One particular moment stands out in my memory during the aftermath of the floods. It was a deeply confronting experience when we arrived at a certain apartment block. As we knocked on the door, we were met by a group of flood refugees - families who had lost their homes completely. I remember one woman of South Asian descent answer the door, and just beyond was her presumed family who had been rendered homeless by the flood. We provided them with emergency contact numbers which brought a glimmer of relief to their faces. However, as I walked away from that encounter, I couldn't help but feel heavy and taken aback by the magnitude of their loss. For the longest time, I could still recognise that woman.

Despite being exposed to various shocking scenes throughout the flood crisis, this particular moment still lingers in my mind. It serves as a powerful reminder of the profound impact such natural disasters can have on individuals and communities. Witnessing the devastation and realising that it could easily have been me or someone I know evokes a sense of empathy and compassion within me. It reinforces the importance of coming together as a community and supporting those in need during times of crisis.

As the sun began to set, marking the end of our arduous journey, we boarded the bus. Exhausted but filled with a sense of accomplishment, we engaged in conversations, including discussions about American football, which provided a temporary reprieve from the weight of the day's experiences. Returning to the campus, I reflected on the significance of our efforts and hoped that the people we encountered during our volunteer work received the assistance and support they needed to begin rebuilding their lives.

In these moments, I was constantly reminded about my time in Papua New Guinea. However, there was one simple similarity that I forgot about at the time but believe deserves mention. Such volunteering in service to the greater community was akin to the diggers in Milne Bay.

To the sweating, exhausted volunteers, each new day seemed beyond endurance, yet they continued to endure and work without complaint. In words similar to those of Major General Cyril Clowes, I wish to place on record my appreciation of the magnificent efforts on the part of our volunteers. The success of the operations was in great measure due to their untiring and courageous work. Also, just like Corporal John French, we don't know the worth of quiet people until they are called upon to do something big. Like Maiogura, many of my fellow volunteers would give thanks that they were able, in some small measure, to assist their Australian friends.

On Friday, I teamed up in Pimlico with a middle-aged gentleman from Montana. Time has faded his name from my memory. Throughout our walk we engaged in lively conversations with a particular focus on the Marias Pass, where they had come from. Surprisingly, I had a good understanding of it from my earlier days thanks to *Microsoft Train Simulator*. It was a fascinating topic that kept us engaged as we made our way through the streets. Cavendish Street comes to mind, where we witnessed a mix of ongoing restoration efforts and deserted apartment blocks.

The scorching heat and humidity of the day intensified the challenging conditions we faced. The temperatures remained consistently in the high thirties, causing utter madness. I longed for a refreshing cold shower upon returning home, only to be met with an unexpected hurdle. The pipes had become so heated that even the water from the cold tap turned scorching hot. It served as a testament to the heatwave that engulfed us during that time. However, my American companions and I supported each other like helper diesel engines working together to navigate a heavy freight train through the treacherous Marias Pass in the midst of a winter storm.

Saturday saw me join a team in Hermit Park, navigating the streets beyond the various stores of Charters Towers Road. Philp, Marks, and Armstrong Streets stood out in particular. Anna was leading the way. I didn't think our paths would cross again that soon. I especially didn't think it would be during another volunteering in a tropical marathon like Papua New Guinea. Our job of communicating was made easier by the fact I still had her in my Facebook contacts. Because you never know…

One sight that day I remember rather well was a spillway that had collected a lot of stuff in it. It served as a reminder that the whole ordeal was not done yet. It was still raining softly that day too. Near the end, we rested at a picnic table in Summerfield Street. The makeshift rubbish dump at Lou Litster Park was a hundred meters away with bulldozers and workers still clearing it, part by part.

That day, our individual coverage of the suburb was quite thorough. It's worth noting that some dedicated half the day to a shift, while some went from 8am-5pm. I can't remember which ones I went for on each day, but I sure took the long option when I could. I knew I could push through and endure such a volunteering challenge thanks to the lessons learned from other volunteer jobs.

By the end of the week, our job was finally complete, and it was a moment of profound relief and satisfaction. The collective effort had been nothing short of incredible, showcasing the true spirit of community among all those who volunteered. Regardless of which group or organisation they were affiliated with, every single volunteer played a crucial role in this monumental task. From coordinating logistics to distributing supplies, each contribution was a vital piece of the puzzle.

As I reflected on the week's events, I felt a deep sense of exhaustion wash over me, a physical reminder of the hard work and dedication that had gone into our efforts. Yet, despite my fatigue, there was an undeniable sense of accomplishment and pride in knowing that my contributions had made a meaningful impact. I had helped my fellow residents of Townsville on their road to recovery, a journey that many are still navigating.

The aftermath of the situation had left its mark on our community, and it was clear that the recovery process would be ongoing for some time. I watched as neighbours came together, sharing stories and supporting one another, each individual carrying their own burdens while also lifting each other up. It was a powerful testament to resilience and unity, reminding me that even in the face of adversity, we are stronger together. Each small act of kindness and support added up, creating a ripple effect that would help our town heal and rebuild. I felt fortunate to be part of such a remarkable community, one that continues to rise and support each other in times of need.

That was the end of my volunteer story for that February. There was a second phase of the Team Townsville volunteering, and I was willing to do that, however, it was not to be. I later learned that that phase was not as big or difficult as the previous one. Therefore, the YWAM volunteers in that one did not require additional help for it.

Nonetheless, I am still proud of what I did achieve. Together as one, we would not be broken. We at Team Townsville have done a tremendous job in ensuring the mental and physical wellbeing of the disaster victims and a gradual recovery of our fallen communities. The stories of our missions will be told by us for ages to come. I, for one, will make sure of that. Of course, mine wasn't the only story of the team. I'm sure there are many other fellow volunteers out there with their own stories. I hope that their experiences were shared in some form.

Now that the floods had subsided, a new chapter in the aftermath began. It was important to recognise that the term "post-disaster" encompassed a lengthy period, one that could extend indefinitely. The road to recovery would be challenging and require ongoing efforts. The effects of the floods would linger, presenting numerous obstacles to overcome, but we were determined to face them head-on. The resilience of the community was evident as people came together to rebuild their lives and their city. It was a steady journey forward, marked by small victories and incremental progress. The damage caused by the floods would not be easily erased, and many challenges would persist for an extended period of time. Infrastructure needed repair, homes needed rebuilding, and emotional wounds needed healing.

But amid the difficulties, there was a spirit of unity and duty that carried us forward. Support and assistance poured in from various organisations, volunteers, and government agencies. Community initiatives were launched to provide aid and resources to those in need. The strength and solidarity of the people of Townsville shone through as they supported one another and worked towards a common goal.

The recovery process extended beyond physical repairs and restoration. Emotional and psychological healing was also crucial. Many individuals and families had experienced profound loss and trauma. It was important to provide ongoing support and resources for their well-being, ensuring that no one was left behind in the journey towards recovery.

While the road ahead would be long and challenging, we were committed to persevering. We had witnessed the strength of the human spirit in the face of adversity, and we knew that together we could overcome any obstacles that lay in our path. The floods had tested us, but they had also brought out the best in us.

As we moved forward, we carried the lessons learned from the floods, the bonds forged through shared experiences, and the commitment to build a stronger, more resilient community. The aftermath of the floods would remain a part of our collective memory, a reminder of the challenges we had overcome, and the strength we had discovered within ourselves.

The journey of recovery would continue, and we would remain steadfast in our commitment to rebuild, heal, and thrive. The floods had left their mark, but they had not defeated us. Together, we would forge a brighter future, ensuring that Townsville would emerge from this disaster stronger and more resilient than ever before.

As I wrote about these people of Townsville rebuilding their lives in the aftermath of the floods, I couldn't help but think of something I encountered in my readings: the unique art form of Kintsugi. This renowned Japanese art form involves repairing broken pottery by filling the cracks with gold. What was once considered damaged and unusable is now restored in a way that highlights the imperfections rather than hiding them. The cracks, once flaws, now become the very thing that makes the piece unique, beautiful, and valuable. In Kintsugi, the process of mending doesn't erase the past, but instead transforms it. The pottery, which might have been discarded as broken, is not only made whole again, but is made even more precious and beautiful than before.

I first learned about this metaphor in Demi Tebow's autobiography, *A Crown That Lasts*. I later explored it in greater detail in Sandra Hubert's deeply personal account, *I'll Do It Myself*, of rebuilding her life after a serious brain injury, the launch of which my mother and I attended. In these stories, as well as the eponymous song by *Moonlight Haze*, I began to understand that Kintsugi is more than just an art form. It's a philosophy that can be applied to our own lives.

And in a way, that's exactly what I saw happening in the aftermath of the flood in Townsville. The people, much like the broken pottery, were picking up the shattered pieces of their lives and rebuilding, but not just to restore them to their original state. Through the hardship, the struggle, and the healing process, they became stronger, more valuable, and more beautiful than they had been before. The cracks, the scars left behind by the floods, didn't make them weaker; they became the symbols of resilience, the markers of what they had survived and overcome.

What's remarkable is that we all have the potential to do this in our own lives. Through our struggles, we have the opportunity to reframe our hardships and brokenness, seeing them not as obstacles, but as catalysts for growth. Each challenge we face, each pain we endure, can shape us into something more. When we view our trauma and pain through this lens, we no longer feel defined by our brokenness. Instead, we begin to see our scars as marks of strength. And as we share our stories and embrace the journey of healing, we move from being broken to becoming unbreakable.

Just like the art of Kintsugi, we learn that there is beauty in the cracks. The gold that fills those spaces doesn't just restore us, it elevates us. It's through healing and growth that we discover the true value of who we've become. And that, as the metaphor goes, is what makes us whole again.

Chapter Ten

When the Waters Withdrew

Years have passed since the floods. Now, we have seen disasters that far exceed them in severity and impact. We've seen the Black Summer fires and their almost inconceivably horrible effects. I remember seeing the images of the burning landscapes. They were visions of hell. Barely a year since the floods, the fires had destroyed nearly four times more homes.

The fires primarily affected the states of New South Wales, Victoria, and South Australia, though nearly every state experienced some degree of impact. Approximately 18.6 million hectares were destroyed, making it one of the largest fires ever recorded globally. At least 33 people died, including firefighters, and many more suffered injuries. Additionally, smoke-related illnesses were estimated to have caused over 400 deaths when, at its peak, air quality dropped to hazardous levels in all southern and eastern states. It is estimated that more than 3 billion animals were affected, with species like koalas suffering significant population losses. The fires caused immense damage to habitats, leading to fears that some species may face extinction.

Three thousand homes were destroyed. The fires caused an estimated AUD $103 billion in economic losses, factoring in damage to infrastructure, tourism, and healthcare. The smoke generated by the fires created a public health crisis with Sydney, Canberra, and other cities experiencing hazardous air quality levels for weeks. Smoke from the fires even drifted as far as South America. The environmental toll was immense, with vast stretches of bushland, forest, and national parks ravaged. The fires released 400 million tons of CO_2 into the atmosphere.

Seeing that on the news and social media was incredibly disheartening. The many photos of the smoke from space and the flames rising high were images I'll never forget. The detailed stories of the many affected communities were horrific. Finally, the amount of ignorant blame-deflecting and finger-pointing by politicians and their admiring media personalities was depressing. The disregard and ridiculing of scientific consensus by some of the Newscorp tabloids was something I despised to watch. Such hyperbole is no comfort for the affected people who saw hell manifest in their hometowns.

Despite what they said, climate change and long-term drought conditions played a significant role, with Australia experiencing its hottest and driest year on record. These conditions created an environment ripe for the rapid spread of fires. The Indian Ocean Dipole contributed to unusually dry conditions, and strong winds helped the fires grow out of control.

That said, this larger natural disaster was met with a larger volunteering force. Reinforcements from all over Australia were called in to assist fighting the fires and relieve exhausted local crews in New South Wales. The Australian Defence Force was again mobilised, this time to provide air support to the firefighting effort and to provide manpower and logistical support in the blood red sky. Firefighters, supplies, and equipment came in from Canada, New Zealand, Singapore, and the United States among others, to help fight the fires. While wounded then, the Australian spirit is something that will never be broken. Our unity, duty, and destiny would persist on.

A significant amount of government funding and resources were directed toward recovery efforts, including mental health support for affected communities, and wildlife recovery programs. A Royal Commission was established to examine Australia's preparedness and response to the bushfires, looking into causes such as climate change, land management, and firefighting resources. Rebuilding efforts are still ongoing with calls for better fire management practices and stronger action on climate change to prevent future disasters of this scale.

The 2020 Black Summer fires were a wake-up call for Australia. Therefore, we should remember it as such.

As 2020 progressed, the time later would be marked by the far-reaching impact of the Covid-19 pandemic, reshaping lives and communities globally. As Queensland, like many regions, faced the challenges of lockdowns, the Community Information Centre, a hub for volunteering, temporarily closed its doors to protect the vulnerable volunteers, many of whom were elderly. During this time, my focus shifted to safeguarding my grandmother, and recognising her vulnerability was a top priority within our family.

In response to the pandemic, I joined the ranks of the immunised, viewing it as a crucial step to contribute to the safety of my community, city, and the broader population. Disregarding the ignorance of a vocal minority, I emphasised the importance of collective efforts, understanding that too much had already been lost at this point.

The resilience and spirit of volunteers emerged prominently during the local sector of the pandemic, showcasing the power of coming together in times of crisis.

Amidst the uncertainties, I extended my support to friends and family, both locally and abroad, checking in on their well-being during the lockdown. The hope remained that our combined efforts, bolstered by the indomitable spirit of volunteers, would be sufficient to navigate through these challenging times without enduring significant loss of life. It is a testament to the strength of communities and individuals when faced with adversity, underscoring the importance of solidarity and shared responsibility in safeguarding the well-being of all.

Prior to the outbreak in Queensland, Team Townsville was rising again. The next phase was an advertising stand. For this, they had a briefing at the CIC which I attended. The plan they had laid out was a pretty decent one. The first one that I went to was a small weekend event in Corcoran Park, Pimlico. A fair amount of merchandise was handed out, including a storm preparedness guide, wrist bands, and stress balls. There was also a foldable paper house that doubled as a money bank that the kids could put money in to reserve for an emergency. Pimlico had many houses that were affected by the floods, and its community had gathered for this little event. Some had stories to tell. Some were looking on the bright side, some were left emotional. Their predicament had not yet finished...

Unfortunately, the first virus outbreak severely hampered our ability to continue that sort of engagement. For the remainder of when they were active, I did not hear back from them concerning any future events. I still have the polo shirt that bears their name, as do others. Now, the funding and operations of Team Townsville have ceased. Or, as I like to say, its mission has been accomplished.

A TIME FOR VOLUNTEERS

While the operations of Team Townsville have ceased, it's important to recognise the positive impact they had during their active period. Their mission of raising awareness and providing resources for storm preparedness was accomplished, leaving a lasting impression on the community. The polo shirt bearing their name serves as a reminder of their efforts and the resilience of the Townsville community.

Even though circumstances have changed, it's crucial for individuals to continue prioritising preparedness and staying informed about potential hazards. The experience and knowledge gained from events like the floods and the work of organisations like Team Townsville can serve as a foundation for future readiness and response efforts.

As the community moves forward, it's essential to remember the spirit of unity and support that emerged during challenging times. Together, Townsville can continue to build resilience and face any future challenges with a shared commitment to the well-being of its residents.

Over time, I've heard multiple flood-affected people vent their anger at many things. I have heard them be called many things. I'd rather not take sides or endorse any such views in this story. In the end, though, there is nothing I can do about that. It's understandable that during times of disaster and hardship, emotions can run high, and frustrations with insurance companies may arise. While it's important to acknowledge and respect the experiences and perspectives of flood-affected individuals, it's also crucial to maintain a balanced view and avoid generalisations.

In times of disaster, it becomes even more vital for communities to come together and support each other. Unity and collaboration are key in overcoming challenges and rebuilding. It's essential to focus on fostering a sense of solidarity and understanding, rather than allowing divisions to deepen. Ultimately, the strength of a community lies in its ability to unite and support one another during difficult times. By coming together, sharing experiences, and working towards common goals, communities can overcome adversity and build a more resilient future. Fears, like the misinformation that propels them, are simply illusions.

Over time, I discovered other avenues to help out, even in the midst of a lockdown. It was that time of year again; The Extra Life stream event, made possible by the Children's Miracle Network Hospitals, was about to kick off, and what a perfect moment to hold it. I connected with my friends, Sam Jones and David Hammer, in our Discord group, ready to rally together for a cause that transcended our circumstances. On Game Day, our goal was clear: to raise money for children's hospitals and support the young ones who needed it most.

As I stood on the beaches of Bowen that day, I entered a thoughtful state of mind in the clear, bright scene. The sky was a deep, vivid blue, contrasting beautifully with the turquoise sea. The gentle waves rippled towards the sandy shore where large rocks dotted the landscape. The distant hills on the horizon were visible under the sun, while a vibrant green shrubbery bordered the beach, bringing life and contrast to the simplicity. It's an inviting and peaceful daytime beach scene, perfect for a relaxing escape. In the sanctuary of my father's friend's house in this area, I have witnessed many things from the screen and then retired to the nearby beach to reflect, deep in thought. Today was no exception, but rather a prime example.

Gazing out at the endless expanse of the ocean during my recent journey, I began to think about how to articulate the importance of this event. That year posed numerous challenges for all of us. Here in Australia, we had not been spared from hardship. We started the year with our country engulfed in flames, facing bushfires that left scars on our land and communities that would take years, if not decades, to heal. The challenges didn't end there; the pandemic swept through, and with it came a wave of misinformation and division that threatened to tear us apart. By that point, over a million lives had been lost, and the anger brewing among us seemed to poison our unity. Hunger and desperation eroded our sense of duty, while fear held us back from embracing our potential.

Perhaps most concerning to me was the growing sense of resignation, a pervasive feeling that many were giving up hope. Some voices echoed the sentiment that there was no point in fighting back, no purpose in striving for a better world.

So, I asked: Was this what we truly wanted? To surrender and accept our fate? To anyone who thought that way, I said: No.

Sure, we had been dealt heavy blows. But it wasn't about how hard we had been hit; it was about our resilience; about how hard we could be struck and still move forward. That was how we achieved victory. This dark period was temporary, though it might have lasted another year, five years, or even a decade. There was no guarantee that 2021 would be any better, and personally, it wouldn't be for me. Yet I firmly believed that eventually, this would subside. However, if we chose to give up, that pain would last forever.

We had to believe that change was possible. We might have stumbled, but we would not fall like this. This Extra Life event was much more than just an annual charity drive; it represented a beacon of hope for the children who would inherit this world. It was an opportunity to give them a better chance at life and empower them as the next generation. This event allowed us to spread love and joy in a world often overshadowed by hate and despair. It was a chance for our community to unite and sing in one voice, a collective expression of hope and resilience. Together, we demonstrated that, even in the face of adversity, we could uplift one another and inspire change. We came together to show that hope, kindness, and compassion were stronger than the challenges we faced.

That saga continued to unfold every year, evolving with each new chapter. In 2021, I joined Sam and his friends amid a tremendous thunderstorm, the heavy rain and booming thunder creating an exhilarating, adrenaline-pumping atmosphere as we engaged in our war simulator battles. The storm added a layer of intensity to our gaming, making each moment feel electric as we strategized and fought together, fuelled by our shared mateship.

The following year, 2022, marked a new milestone for me. I set up my brand-new gaming PC and streamed from home, feeling a wave of excitement wash over me as I prepared to join the event. Later in the week, I watched the Rooster Teeth livestream from Bowen where it perfectly coincided with a beautiful sunny day. The sun rose over the stunning cliffsides and pristine beaches during it. The colours ranged from deep orange near the horizon, blending into soft yellows and light blues as the sky brightened. The sun had yet to fully rise above the horizon, casting a warm, golden glow on the water, which reflected the morning light. In 2023, I found myself watching the event from home once more, but in hindsight it carried a bittersweet weight. It was the last time I would witness the Rooster Teeth Extra Life event, as Rooster Teeth Productions was set to shut down in 2024.

Despite that, I knew my Extra Life journey was far from over. The spirit of community and compassion that had driven us to raise money for children's hospitals remained alive in my heart. I recognised that whatever came next, I would be there.

My stays in Bowen are always a time for self-reflection. Walking alone on the beach that night, I saw the moon low on the horizon, casting a soft glow across the water's surface. The reflection of the moonlight formed a shimmering path, stretching toward the foreground, while the dark silhouettes of distant landmasses added depth. Their presence and the sea beyond were a reminder that there was always something more on the horizon. The sky was clear except for a few scattered clouds, which created subtle variations in the light. The calmness of the water and the serene atmosphere gave a peaceful, almost surreal quality. The overall effect was one of tranquil beauty, highlighting the natural landscape at dusk. Yet, there is a sombreness as well, I feel, in being alone partaking in such a sight. I had come far in this massive land and vowed to continue doing so.

There was a lot more to reflect on, for while all of that was happening, so were many other things...

Chapter Eleven

Volunteering Beyond

Since the floods, my life has continued on its trajectory. I remained dedicated to volunteering at CIC, contributing to their growth and development. Simultaneously, I pursued my academic endeavours, resuming my studies at Central Queensland University. Building on the foundation laid during the completion of the Diploma of Aviation in 2017, my flight training commenced in 2020, propelling me into new adventures within the realm of aviation.

To commemorate the events and heroes of the floods, I acquired a "Floody Legends" shirt, a symbolic token available through the Townsville Bulletin. This garment serves as a visual tribute, listing the various groups that played pivotal roles during the disaster including the Australian Defence Force, Queensland Police, Queensland Fire and Emergency Service, Townsville Local Disaster Management Group, Red Cross, State Emergency Service, Townsville City Council, Queensland Rural Fire Service, Ergon Energy, local media, Townsville Tinnie Army, and all the local community heroes. The shirt's imagery on the front depicts an ASLAV ploughing through the floods, accompanied by an SES boat and a Tinnie Army boat, a powerful representation of the collaborative efforts that unfolded during those challenging times. As anniversary articles resurface, I urge everyone to read them and, above all, lend an attentive ear to the narratives of those directly affected for their recollections are paramount.

Believing in the cyclical nature of disaster stories, I am confident that in the next tale of adversity, a new cadre of heroes will emerge, perhaps another Tinnie Army, Ute Army, Off-Road Army, or even a Hovercraft Army for all I know. Whether in the water, on the ground, or in the air, these heroes will navigate through fire, rain, wind, or cold, always finding their place within the narrative. As demonstrated in the floods, their actions will be defined by a commitment to doing what is necessary, within the realm of what is possible, and executed with a keen understanding of how it should be done.

Meanwhile, the narrative of my volunteering journey took an unexpected turn around mid-2021, a period marked by a confluence of anxiety, stress from a sudden study load, and the weight of a significant personal tragedy. In the dimly lit common room on campus, a moment etched in memory for the wrong reasons, I made a pivotal phone call to the CIC. It was then that I communicated the necessity to put my volunteering commitments on hold, a decision that eventually led to an end of my involvement altogether.

It's a moment that hurts my heart to remember...

The final chapter of my time there unfolded during Volunteering Week when we all embarked on a visit to Magnetic Island. The acknowledgment from the ferry's skipper, echoing our dedication over the ship's PA system, became an unexpected yet heartening farewell. The day's culmination at the markets on Horseshoe Bay was followed by personal reflection time alone. When I first started volunteering, it was during a time I was lost in life, essentially. Wandering around looking for something to do with no employment, study, or steady progress. But now, I have found study again and with it, a new goal over new horizons to continue striving for.

In the midst of the tumultuous period marked by upheaval and personal challenges, a glimmer of opportunity emerged. A paid part-time administrative role at Volunteering North Queensland materialised, offering a potential respite and a chance to contribute once more to the community that had been a vital part of my journey. The application process unfolded with an unexpected smoothness, culminating in a successful outcome.

Come October, the winds of change swept in. I found myself back in the workforce, donning the mantle of a part-time administrative role. This role not only provided a steady anchor during a time of personal turbulence but also afforded me the privilege of giving back to the community that had been a steadfast source of support and inspiration throughout my journey.

Top of Form

Throughout my time there, I saw and did many things from my place at the front desk. My first memory of Volunteering North Queensland was watching the Melbourne Cup from the office, a moment of excitement and mateship that broke the usual routine. I remember Jacqui warmly welcoming me and guiding me through my duties, patiently teaching me how to navigate the various software platforms we used to streamline our business operations. I became adept at processing records and managing the flow of information, while Microsoft Excel became my go-to tool for arranging and analysing the data we collected from our volunteer network. Once the daily tasks were complete, I would tidy up the space, ensuring that everything was in order before I called it a day.

A TIME FOR VOLUNTEERS

Some days, I would step outside the office and be greeted by the warm afternoon sun, other days by the sudden crash of thunderstorms that are so familiar in North Queensland. Regardless of the weather, I had a routine, heading home to relax and reflect on the day's work, usually listening to audiobooks through my car's Bluetooth. The voices of narrators, with their distinct tones and styles, became a comforting presence on those drives, a way to unwind after the challenges of the day.

Jacqui would move on to greater things, and Erin would take her place. She was a hard-working boss indeed. Her leadership, enhanced by intriguing, storied past experience, would show over time. She steered VNQ through all sorts of challenges and achievements.

Beyond the office, my involvement in the broader volunteering community took me on various adventures. I remember participating in Extra Life while I was in Bowen, a gaming marathon for charity that added a new layer to my understanding of what it means to give back. It was more than just traditional volunteering; it was fun, digital, and a great way to make a difference through something I loved. That experience gave me a sense of purpose, connecting with others for a good cause, even if we were miles apart.

At the end of the year, I took on a new role as the Scribe at the Stable on the Strand nativity event which was hosted for the first time at Riverway. It was such a unique experience, stepping into character and becoming a part of a live retelling of one of the most well-known stories in history. There was a certain magic in the air during the event, with families gathered to celebrate, children wide-eyed with wonder, and volunteers working hard to bring it all to life. It was a rewarding way to close the year, surrounded by a strong sense of community.

Then, 2021 gave way to 2022 and I found myself welcoming the new year with a sense of relief and optimism. I was so glad for the fresh start, feeling that after the challenges of the previous year, this was an opportunity to move forward, to grow, and to continue making a positive impact both within Volunteering North Queensland and beyond. It was the beginning of another chapter in my journey, filled with new possibilities, new lessons, and, of course, new stories to tell.

The VNQ Conference and Awards was a truly proud moment for me. It began with a series of speeches and presentations at the Council building where the air was filled with anticipation and excitement. The main conference took place in the corporate box of the Queensland Country Bank Stadium, a venue I had never imagined I would find myself in. As I looked through the large glass windows overlooking the stadium, I felt a rush of awe. The electronic billboard was a striking sight, displaying an event advertisement with vibrant graphics, our logo showcased prominently in grand scale.

Inside the corporate box, I noticed several individuals seated at a table representing various organisations. They appeared to be engaged in a deep discussion or preparing materials, hinting that this was an integral part of the conference activities. The atmosphere was charged with energy as everyone prepared for the event, reinforcing the significance of our collective mission.

The experience escalated further with the Volunteer Awards Night, hosted at the Quayside Terminal. Dressed in my finest suit, I felt a wave of pride as I entered the venue which was filled with an air of celebration. Glenn "Minty" Mintern took on the role of MC, bringing his charisma and showmanship to the occasion. Throughout the night, we were treated to a series of inspiring videos that showcased the invaluable contributions of volunteers to our city. All the while, I engaged in lively conversations with attendees from volunteer organisations all over the region.

This evening was a pinnacle moment during my time as a member of that community, a celebration of dedication and service that left a lasting impression on me. I had hardly known a moment grander than that night, which not only recognised the hard work of so many but also served as a reminder of the impact we could have when we came together for the greater good.

More travels were in store, from Paluma to Atherton, Herberton, and Mareeba. Herberton in particular serves as a testament to the power of volunteering. The inception of the Historic Village owes its gratitude foremost to the pioneering spirit of Herberton's early settlers, and subsequently, to a lineage of committed inhabitants who followed in their footsteps. Its continuity today is owed to the dedication of two couples: collector, Harry Skennar and his spouse, Ellen, and proprietors, Craig and Connie Kimberley, who, with unwavering support from the local Herberton community, uphold the tradition of preservation and restoration. No endeavour has been deemed too grand or trivial, and their collective aspiration to rejuvenate this captivating attraction has now come to fruition. Boasting over 60 original structures dating back to Herberton's inception as a tin mining hub, every facet of the museum has been meticulously gathered and refurbished. While the primary restoration endeavours have reached completion, ongoing maintenance and vigilant care are indispensable for the upkeep of the buildings and the myriad original artifacts exhibited within and around the Village. Their aspiration remains that visitors will immerse themselves in a full day's exploration, unearthing hidden gems amidst the diverse and splendid collections showcased within the Village's confines.

One of my later memories from those days was listening to the livestream of the Artemis 1 rocket launch on my way back from work. As I drove, the steady voice of the announcer and the building anticipation of the launch filled the car, blending with the hum of the road beneath me. It was a surreal feeling, witnessing such a monumental step in space exploration, even from a distance, while going about my daily routine. That moment was a reminder of how interconnected we all are, from the work we do here on Earth to the vast ambitions we have as a species reaching for the stars.

Unfortunately, for me, it was not to last...

Our organisation, which had been the lifeblood of volunteering in North Queensland for more than three decades, was now facing closure after 33 years of connecting thousands of volunteers with not-for-profit organisations and providing vital training.

Vice-President and Secretary Trayeden Fulmer, President Emily Sehu, and Acting Manager Cayley Downey were quite upset, and eager to express their displeasure. Emily in particular said the heartbreaking decision was made after exhausting all avenues to continue operations. More and more government grants were now funding projects and not the operational side of things, she told the Townsville Bulletin, but how were they supposed to deliver a project if they couldn't even afford to turn on the lights? She also said the closure would be a huge blow to the community and would change the nature of volunteering in Townsville. Groups like VNQ are so important because you want to connect and see your children grow up in a community where people help each other. It would have been a shame to not have a central place wherein people in Townsville could come to find somewhere to volunteer that fits them and get the required training. We all understand that online is the new world, but face to face human contact will still be core to local volunteering. Like most of the people in VNQ, Emily was a volunteer too and knew firsthand how valuable it was for new people in town to be able to find somewhere to connect with others. She said the closure of VNQ would make it

A TIME FOR VOLUNTEERS

harder for people who wanted to volunteer in the region, as well as the network of community groups such as sporting clubs, environmental groups, and aged care services which relied on the organisation.

To that end, a local Channel 7 news camera crew came into the office to gather footage and information for the media release. They hung around for much of the morning, conducting interviews and taking notes. Actually, I remember having a laugh with the journalist about the Channel 7 show, *What Really Happens In Thailand,* which I watched a lot of back in the day. They featured us upfront for 7 News Local at 6PM, featuring B-roll footage with me in it, Cayley being interviewed, and a visual aid of her closing the door – which was a bit of artistic license, since I was the one who usually did that. Additionally, Channel Nine's News at 5:30PM talked about how the "pillar of regional community," as they called us, would be forced to close its doors unless something happened.

This was indeed a noble effort to increase awareness of our plight. Especially since the following morning I would check the VNQ inbox and find messages of sorrow and sympathies for our pending closure. However, as much of a helping hand the newscasts gave us, a slight error in their phrasing made people think that we *were* closing our doors, instead of *about to* close them, which meant we had to convince people that we were still here.

Then, all hope was not lost. It was payback time. As the same Bulletin journalist would write again, there was still hope that Volunteering North Queensland could be brought back from the brink of closure as community members rallied to stop the not-for-profit from folding. Emily said the decision to fold at the end of the year, which was attributed mainly to a lack of funding, was not going to be final anymore after they recently received an outpouring of community support.

However, there was still a catch, The volunteering organisation could continue in another place, but it couldn't have any more paid staff – which included me. It saddened Jacqui to do it, who had taken over again after Erin's resignment, but she announced just that to me shortly after. I understood the situation and was ready to undertake such a parting of ways.

One of my final memories of Volunteering North Queensland was setting up a stand at an event at James Cook University by myself. I was in a booth set up outdoors by the Eddie Koiki Mabo Library under a display tent. A banner was prominently displayed with the organisation's name and services they offer, including referrals, support, training, resources, and information. A former manager at VNQ was in the tent next to me and he was a pleasure to chat with. On the table beneath the tent, several pamphlets, brochures, and small promotional items were arranged, providing information about volunteering opportunities and resources available to the public. There was no better place for this than the green, tree-filled park, with a bright, sunny atmosphere. Beyond, a modern pavilion could be seen, featuring vertical green slats and a seating area which complemented the natural environment.

Then, I finally closed the doors one last time and walked off into the wider world again. It was a strange feeling, leaving behind the familiarity of that space and the people I'd worked with for so long. But with every ending comes a new beginning.

So, what did I do to mark the end of that era? Well, naturally, I celebrated in style with an *Alestorm* and *Valhalore* concert, followed by *Sabaton* at the Good Things Festival. The thunderous energy of live music, surrounded by fellow fans, was the perfect way to let loose and embrace the change ahead. The festival was electric, filled with the heavy riffs of pirate-themed anthems and powerful, historical storytelling, and it felt like the perfect way to end an era.

That, combined with another Stable at Riverway event and a peaceful holiday at Mission Beach really brought that chapter of my life to a close. It was a time of reflection, celebration, and the anticipation of what lay ahead as I stepped forward with a sense of fulfillment and excitement for the future.

Chapter Twelve

Farewell, Olden Ways

The departure from Volunteering North Queensland marked a transition, catapulting me back into the expansive realm of the wider world. Embarking on the quest for employment once again, I found myself navigating the unpredictable currents of change. As I reflect on these experiences while penning these words, a wave of nostalgia washes over me, evoking the mateship and fascination that volunteering brought into my life.

The future, a canvas yet to be painted, unfolds with uncertainties. The path ahead remains uncharted, offering both the allure of endless possibilities and the challenge of navigating the unknown. What lies beyond this juncture is a narrative waiting to be written, an unwritten chapter filled with potential and discovery. The nostalgia serves not as a yearning for the past but as a reminder of the resilience, adaptability, and growth cultivated during those days of volunteering.

As I step forward into the unknown, I carry with me the lessons, memories, and connections forged through the lens of volunteering.

A TIME FOR VOLUNTEERS

The journey continues, and while the destination may be uncertain, the experiences woven into the fabric of my past offer a compass guiding me forward. The pages of my story remain open, waiting to be written with each step I take into the unfolding chapters of the future.

In the ebb and flow of life, I found myself slipping once more into the realm of wandering and uncertainty, a familiar terrain from the challenges faced in 2018. The pressing question echoed: where would I go from here? In the midst of this existential inquiry, a beacon emerged; Writing, my lifelong passion and source of joy. The prospect of immersing myself in the world of words sounded promising, a comforting anchor amid the sea of ambiguity.

In 2023, an unexpected opportunity materialised, offering a chance to venture abroad once again. Taiwan beckoned, and I eagerly seized the opportunity to meet authors James Rosone and Miranda Watson. From the vibrant streets of New Taipei City to the majestic mountains around Hualien and the bustling port of Kaohsiung, the journey unfolded as a story of learning and discovery. Each location etched itself onto my list of places explored, contributing to the mosaic of my experiences. The return journey, also weaving through Hong Kong and Sydney, was not just a physical homecoming to Townsville but a metaphorical one as well.

Armed with newfound confidence and a rekindled desire to pursue my passion for writing, I returned to Townsville. The odyssey through Taiwan had not only added another destination to my travel repertoire but had also reignited the flames of creative inspiration. With a renewed sense of purpose, I embraced the unpredictability of the journey ahead, knowing that within the world of writing, I had found a compass to navigate the uncertainties and turn them into narrative adventures.

But all of that is a story for another time...

During my travels in the meantime, I have witnessed many compelling examples of volunteering in action, each revealing the profound impact individuals can have on their communities…

Joining a tour group for the Avalon Airshow in 2023, I had the opportunity to explore the stunning restorations from every era of aviation housed within the Moorabbin Air Museum, just before the show commenced. The museum was a treasure trove of history, showcasing a wide array of aircraft that painted a vivid picture of aviation's evolution over the years. Each exhibit told a story and I found myself captivated by the craftsmanship and dedication that went into restoring these magnificent flying machines.

On the morning of the airshow, our group made a brief stop at the B-24 Liberator Restoration Museum. Stepping inside, I saw the only remaining Consolidated B-24 Liberator bomber in the Southern Hemisphere, one of only eight still in existence worldwide out of an approximate 18,500 produced. The aircraft stood as a monument to the ingenuity and resilience of its American designers and manufacturers, and I felt a sense of reverence as I walked around its imposing frame. The restoration work was being carried out meticulously in one of the impressive World War II hangars located on the old Werribee airfield just outside Melbourne. Their goal was clear: to eventually restore the airframe to its former glory. The task ahead was monumental, requiring immense patience and dedication to source and assemble parts for the four-engine heavy bomber which had weathered decades of time.

However, as we've seen, the power of volunteering and the drive to see change can overcome any obstacle. It is my imaginative hope that the magnificent machine takes flight and soars over Victoria once more; That there will be a time where the fully restored B-24 Liberator stands proudly in its hangar, gleaming with a fresh coat of olive drab paint; Where the Pratt & Whitney R-1830-35 Twin Wasp engines roar to life, spinning the three-bladed Hamilton Standard propellers as the Liberator begins to taxi, the massive aircraft rolling smoothly across the runway. It then surges ahead, the engines roaring with power and echoing through the airfield as the massive aircraft accelerates down the runway, gaining speed with every passing second. Then, with a gentle lift, the B-24 breaks free from the earth. Soaring upward into the brilliant blue sky, its wings outstretched like a mighty bird reclaiming its domain. With the horizon stretching endlessly before it, the B-24 Liberator flies over the landscape, a symbol of resilience and revival. It is more than just an aircraft; it is a celebration of history, a tribute to the volunteers who pour their hearts into its restoration, and a reminder that even the most daunting challenges can be overcome through dedication and teamwork.

Then, there's the Avalon Airshow itself: a monumental event that words can hardly capture in full detail. So much effort went into bringing it to life, with contributions from numerous organisations, from local councils to defence agencies, working tirelessly behind the scenes to make everything run smoothly. The dedication and coordination made it possible for the skies to be filled with awe-inspiring performances from the Australian Defence Force, the United States Air Force, and international partners like the Japan Air Self-Defence Force, various NATO air forces, and especially the ROK Air Force Black Eagles. The precision of stunt planes left the crowds breathless, while the historic warbirds reminded everyone of the legacy of aviation.

Alongside these incredible aerial feats, displays from defence contractors and aviation groups showcased the latest advancements in military technology and commercial aircraft design. It wasn't just about the performances but about fostering collaboration and innovation between nations and organisations, bringing together both aviation enthusiasts and industry professionals for a spectacle that will be remembered for years to come.

Then, I found myself at the Pacific Airshow on the Gold Coast a few months later and it was a similar story. Just like Avalon, it was a massive effort by countless organisations working together to make it all happen. The shimmering coastline provided a perfect backdrop for high-speed passes from military jets, daring aerobatics from stunt pilots, and flyovers from historic aircraft. It was another celebration of aviation, showcasing the skill, precision, and dedication that had gone into bringing this event to life.

Then came the Pineapple Festival at Rollingstone, a delightful event where I joined the Twin Cities Leos Club to lend a hand to the local Lions group. It was one of those small but charming community gatherings that Queensland is known for, brimming with local pride and tradition. The festival had its own unique flavour, vibrant stalls, live music, and, of course, all things pineapple themed. Next year, I ran into familiar faces from my VNQ days, and we reminisced about past events and efforts, reconnecting over shared memories.

At the turn of said 2024, Tropical Cyclone Kirrily certainly brought forth a remarkable wave of volunteers in the wake of its devastation, and while we've touched upon that extensively throughout this story, it's worth highlighting just how profound the impact of their efforts was. In the aftermath of any cyclone past, communities rallied together, demonstrating an incredible spirit of resilience and solidarity.

During the May Day weekend of 2024, I once again camped up at Lake Tinaroo with friends from the Townsville Sailing Club. We embraced the opportunity to explore the stunning Atherton Tablelands, and I decided to take a scenic drive around Longlands Gap Road to the south and National Highway 1 to the north. As I ventured along

A TIME FOR VOLUNTEERS 185

these picturesque routes, I was reminded of the rich history of the area, and I found myself returning to the Herberton Historic Village once more.

This year, I was excited to discover a new attraction that had taken form from an old relic. There, standing proudly on four wheels, was a restored locomotive labelled "HRM No.1," a small, squat engine that exuded charm and nostalgia. These types of engines were primarily used for short-distance rail services, and often tied to mining or regional transport in the late 19th and early 20th centuries. This model has a well-preserved green paint job with traditional brass and gold accents, a common aesthetic for steam engines of its time. The boiler and chimney are prominent, while the footplate behind the cab appears spacious enough for a driver and fireman. Heritage steam engines such as this are treasured pieces of history, bringing the sights and sounds of a bygone era to modern audiences, often on preserved railways in rural or mountainous regions.

Behind the locomotive was a single old Queensland Rail car painted in a vibrant red and cream. With a piercing whistle and a vigorous chug of steam, the train began its journey in reverse, smoothly making its way toward the Herberton Historic Railway Museum.

The museum, which opened on 20 October 1910, was home to several other collected engines and carriages, each slowly but surely undergoing restoration. I stepped into the railway car, itself a model from old times. The sound of the train chugging along the tracks, combined with the fresh air and beautiful surroundings, created an atmosphere rich with history and the promise of new beginnings.

When I last visited this place in 2021, the locomotive had been parked in the Herberton Railway Workshop, relegated to a silent existence as a museum piece awaiting restoration. At that time, it was a forgotten relic, undergoing meticulous work with the hope of being brought back to life – a Hanger Queen, in aviation terms. I had watched as dedicated volunteers poured their time, patience, and skills into this project, restoring it piece by piece, driven by a shared passion for preserving our history.

Now, seeing it transformed into a functioning train was a testament to their hard work and commitment. The locomotive had finally been granted the chance it so desperately needed, proof that with enough dedication and community support, even the most dormant of treasures could be revitalised. It was a beautiful reminder of how volunteering and a shared vision could breathe new life into the past, connecting generations through the love of history and heritage.

Over time, I myself would continue volunteering for the Townsville State High School ten years after graduation. I would be a member of the P&C for ages. Then, I would take part in the carparking for the V8 Supercars. I would be among those who go out to the school oval with a red traffic wand in hand and guide cars into the parking lot and then out again. Out there, there would be teachers, staff, and others I would know from our meetings. I would sit and chat with them during lulls, and there were also current students I'd chat with, telling them about my time. Other times, I sit and listen to my MP3 player and then audiobooks or the race on the radio. I would take the longest shifts possible since I couldn't think of anywhere better to be. Throughout the years, there would be times when we were called to do parking for other events at Reid Park and even some NRL games in the Townsville Stadium.

I remember one moment I had to put to paper. In 2023, on a sunny afternoon, I sat in under the generous shade of a large tree, just before the outdoor basketball court. I was chatting with Wyatt, an army veteran and member of the school's P&C. Our conversation turned to Papua New Guinea and the military history I had encountered during my time there. When I shared my discoveries, Wyatt told me something that sparked my memory. He spoke of a Japanese soldier who had served in the Second World War and later returned to Rabaul to rekindle his friendship with the local people, so much so that a road had been named in his honour.

That rang a bell from my dives into history. "Is this the man with one arm?" I asked.

"Yes, indeed," Wyatt replied.

That soldier was Shigeru Mura, better known by his pen name, Shigeru Mizuki. Mizuki would go on to become a celebrated manga artist, illustrator, and folklorist. He is most renowned for reviving and popularizing yōkai, supernatural beings from Japanese folklore.

In 1942, Mizuki had been drafted into the Imperial Japanese Army and sent to New Britain Island in Papua New Guinea during their Operation R against Australian defenders in Rabaul. His experiences there left an indelible mark on his soul, from malaria to witnessing the death and suffering of friends to enduring the psychological weight of war. Eventually, during an Allied air raid, he lost his left arm in an explosion. An experience that would later shape his deeply anti-militarist and humanistic works, including Onward Towards Our Noble Deaths.

While recovering in a Japanese field hospital in Rabaul, he was taken in by members of the local Tolai people, who offered him land, a home, and even citizenship via marriage to a Tolai woman. Mizuki seriously considered it. The warmth, generosity, and spiritual calm of the Tolai stood in stark contrast to the war he had just endured. However, a Japanese military doctor convinced him, through shame and duty, to return to Japan for medical treatment.

Though he left, the experience never left him. In interviews, Mizuki later described how his yōkai characters could only appear in times of peace, not war. He gave them no specific ethnicity or nationality – his way of suggesting that humanity, in its purest state, transcends such divisions.

As an author and explorer with my own connection to Papua New Guinea, I found his story both haunting and profoundly moving. The war had taken part of his body, but what he found in the islands gave something back. In that, there's a kind of peace. A bridge between cultures. A road named after a soldier, not for the battles he fought, but for the friendship he kept.

Even as my time in the school faded into history, it felt good to still be coming back. Not only do I give the school something in return, but I also find myself having a part in another of its long running chapters.

All of this would culminate during my attendance of the Townsville State High School's 100th Year Anniversary Gala Dinner on 11 October 2024. Clad in formal attire with my blue suit and a yellow tie with my Seniors 2014 pin on it, I arrived at The Ville, the exact same place I had attended my own formal ten years ago when it was still known as Jupiter's Casino. Making my way across the majestic décor of the pavilion, I would take my seat at Table 1 with graduates from 1994 and beyond. Celebrating with rosé and red wine, I witnessed a video describing the school's long and storied history, with accompanying photos, historic items, and speeches. Many familiar faces from the P&C were also there, as were those from many other eras.

Meanwhile, I saw the new Year 12 graduates about to be released into the world as adults, and I felt many positive feelings. For one, I harken back to when I was in that same position with my own lifelong friends, doing, watching, and listening. I also felt brimming confidence for whatever came our collective way. As they live out some

A TIME FOR VOLUNTEERS

of their greatest moments, come together as friends, and are free to pursue their dreams, another generation of aspiring talents is born. Should disaster strike or loom ahead, there will always be a chosen few youthful talents who will strive for better things. Should the sound of distant thunder be heard once more, they will heed the call for a greater cause.

This I have seen. This I know.

Now we come to late 2024 where I will end this story. Writing this, I have reflected on everything I've experienced, knowing that this is just one story among many. Whatever else I encounter in the future, it will be part of a new tale waiting to be told. For now, this chapter is complete, and anything that lies ahead will be a story for another time.

However, as this story draws to a close, I feel compelled to share one last experience, a personal reflection related to the floods, an encounter that unfolded quietly in the aftermath.

In the waning days of that February, I paid a visit to the Town Common once again. I usually escaped there, when the opportunity came around, to exercise, escape, or just ponder like I did that day. It was here that I had planned for the future on many occasions. I remember bringing Jamie over a few times, who has now returned to America. I'll never forget the stuff we got up to around this city, nor her presence in those troubling times.

The view and the ecosystem at the Common, a quiet corner in a wide regional city, was at least one thing the floods had helped in the long run. From the view of the bird lookout, I saw a serene, natural landscape featuring a calm, reflective body of water surrounded by lush green vegetation. A range of gently rolling hills or small mountains covered in dense green foliage dominated the background. The overcast sky contributed to a soft, muted atmosphere, enhancing the tranquillity of the scene. The surrounding grasslands and patches of tall reeds emphasised the wetland nature of the location, creating a harmonious blend of water and greenery. The peaceful setting evoked a sense of calm, untouched wilderness. Many small lakes were decorating the evergreen field. Pelicans, magpie geese, brolgas, and many other birds were prospering in the newfound water, full of insects to eat. The plants were as green and alive as they could ever be. Further away, the hills were also showing signs of life with their many trees and plants blossoming green.

Then I saw it. In the rustling of the leaves, the blowing of the breeze, and chatter of the animals, I realised all of nature here had recovered. It had adjusted and started anew with the water that it had received. After the storm, the sun was still shining. After the rain, the grass began to grow again. The many inhabitants, big and small, would continue to live their lives. As time progresses, this new land would be their complete home again.

To my fellow volunteers, I say this moment encapsulates the essence of our collective endeavours. Through the challenges we've faced, from the ravages of Cyclone Yasi to the recent floods and the enduring echoes of the World War II air raids, we have stood as a resilient force, unwavering in our commitment to rebuild and uplift communities in their darkest hours. Our efforts are not in vain; they are a beacon that pierces through the darkness, making the night less daunting and empty.

In the grand tapestry of our world, we are but small voices resonating in a vast expanse. Yet, the impact of our collective presence is immeasurable. When challenges arise, volunteers emerge, ready to face adversity head-on and illuminate the path towards recovery.

I have seen this. I know this.

A world with voices proclaiming, "I am here" resonates far louder than a silent world. Each individual voice may seem inconspicuous, but the difference between zero and one is as great as one and infinity.

As we chronicle these experiences, we ensure that our voices will not fade into echoes. It is our responsibility to seek others while there is still time, to weave a chorus of resilience, compassion, and solidarity. In time, the harmony of these voices will reverberate, creating a powerful narrative that transcends the immediate challenges, shaping a future where the echoes of our efforts continue to inspire and uplift those who follow in our footsteps.

New stories await, but old lessons must be remembered. Those lessons will be useful in the next natural onslaught. Be it cyclones, floods, fires, or anything else, there will always be an army of volunteers ready to rise. They showed that our sense of duty does not fall from above. Instead, it is found and remains in corners of the heart.

I feel no concern for them, save for a small one that I hope will be overcome. That being the folks of today, so frightened to change again, may bury their name before long...

Acknowledgements

I extend a big thank you to the people of the Community Information Centre. In the time I've spent with you guys, I have learned so much. It is thanks to you that I was able to gather information about this part of our history, volunteer to help people who have been affected by it and help contribute to ensuring that such a disaster of this magnitude will not be so damaging again. I especially acknowledge Teresa Hudson who helped spread the word of this and encouraged me to go forward.

Special thanks to the Townsville City Library for offering me the opportunity to contribute this story to their platform. I hope this helps you all out greatly with preserving this chapter in our history.

Many thanks, of course, to all the people I've spoken with and interviewed over time. Your own perspectives have helped me acquire as much information as I can concerning this story.

And finally, I offer my sincere gratitude to my friend and writing mentor, Rebeccah Statham. Your teachings and words have inspired me immensely to ignite my spark and go for it. Your words are high praise coming from a best-selling author and friend like you.

To greater things!

From the author

I hope you have enjoyed this book.

I would really value connecting with readers via social media, especially on Instagram at @author.james.byrne. That is where you will see updates on future projects, sights I've seen, and other stories I share. I also have a YouTube channel, @Wedgetail14, which I dedicate most of my creativity towards.

Some videos are particularly relevant to this story. I've even combined footage I took from those days and added it to my fictional video series, "A Wing of Volunteers," and used footage from Papua New Guinea in many more. All of this I dedicate to my community around me. Otherwise, there are various updates, gaming-related videos, travel vlogs, stream highlights, fictional Machinima-style sci-fi videos, and whatever else comes to mind.

As an independent author, reviews are very important to me and make a huge difference to other prospective readers. If you enjoyed this book, I humbly ask you to write up a positive review on Amazon. I sincerely appreciate each person that takes the time to write one.

If you'd like to learn more about disaster recovery in Townsville and stay up to date with warnings, check out the Emergency Management Dashboard at https://disaster.townsville.qld.gov.au/

Take care, stay safe, and remember to plan, prepare, and survive.

Made in the USA
Monee, IL
03 May 2026

49438363R00108